The Future's
Mirror

Cornelia Hesse-Honegger

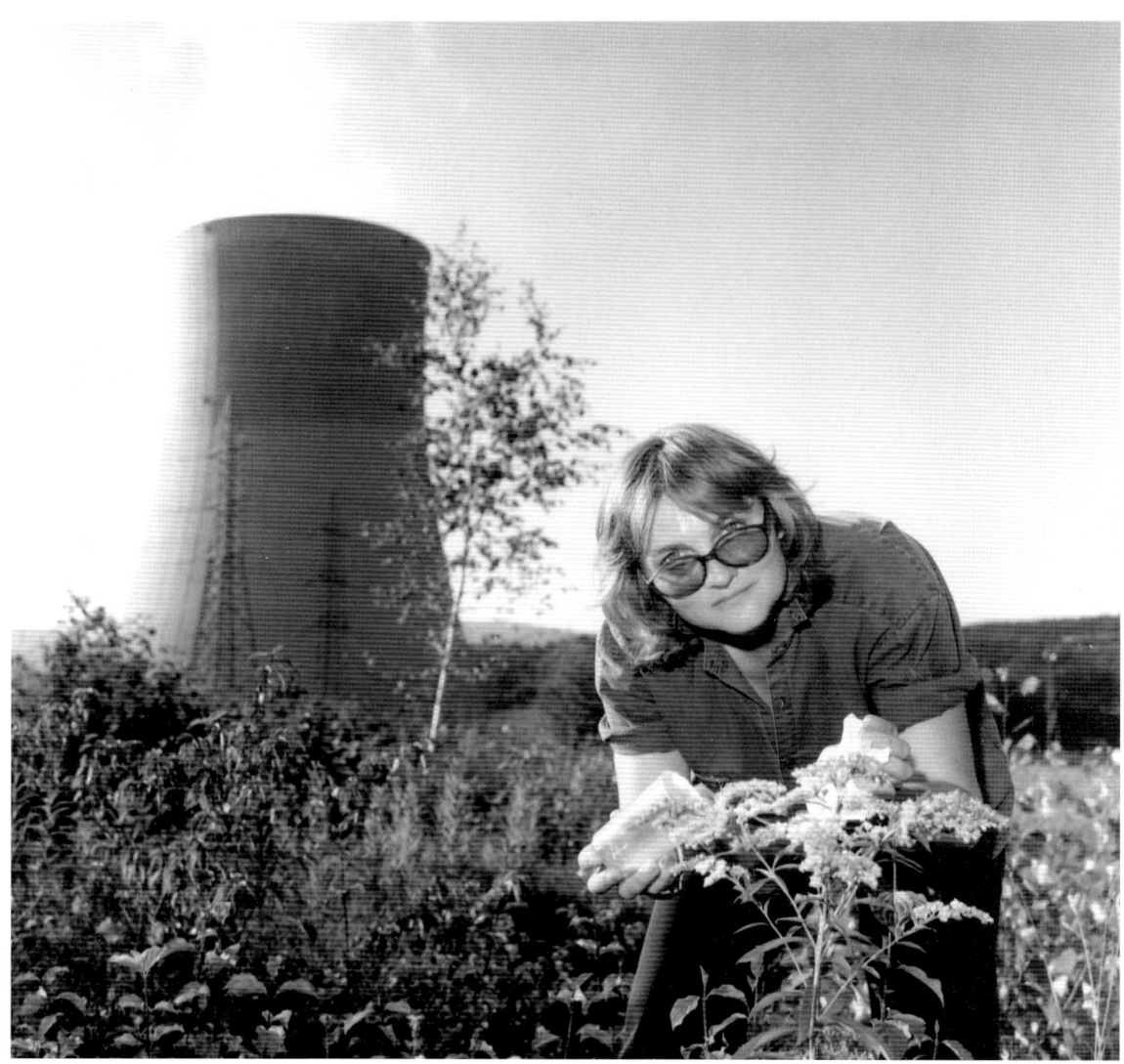

I would like to thank my father Gottfried Honegger, who gave me my artistic training, and the sense to be receptive and strident at the same time. I also wish to thank not only my teachers but the scientists who have opposed my work - they give me the strength to go on.

Above the church upon the hill,
I saw the radiation lab, the arsenal,
and weapons still. The place they
Study war as though Mumbo Jumbo
Had them in his grip,

And I saw no intelligence at all,
Despite technology, and science,
Art, and Newton's law,

I saw their intellects were
Dark and dull as though
No light shone from within.

It dared to call itself a mind,
Yet did not know or see.

A Brontosaurus stood and reared;
A Pteradactyl spread its wings.

Their great unblinking eyes were blind
Just as their mandibles were dumb.

The armored tanks,
The armies clashing in the night,
The antediluvian thing of war,
A remnant of reptilian mind.

And in a flash I saw them already
as extinct,
As something that will pass away,
Just as dark gives way to light at dawn.

And what I saw this time
Was not the thing I'd seen before,
An evil to fight blow for blow,

I saw I must not fight at all
But lay down sword and shield.

Dark Fortress on a Dark Hill
by Sally Abbott

Foreword: The Necessity of Research Beside the Mainstream

by Inge Schmitz-Feuerhake

If one believes the official statements about science, and related speeches, the progress of research cannot exist without the originality and creativity of single personalities; without open-minded thinkers and unconventional ideas. Those who are insiders of academic life know, however, that conventional research operates within strictly defined hierarchies and clearly fenced disciplines, wherein there is no encouragement or development of a sense of deviation. The tremendous wealth of information available to us promotes, by necessity, a high grade of specialisation, and a consequent inability to recognise approaches which lie beyond these boundaries. No wonder then that this system is unable to adequately recognise threats to our natural environment, let alone achieve solutions. Those scientists who make demands for the creation of a new series of concerns are generally excluded by this system.

Bioindicators form a key component of environmental research. Most of them are useful only if the contaminations they contain are already high, or the defects already obvious. Cornelia Hesse-Honegger began her scientific work in the good old tradition of scientific researchers: by systematic and precise observation. Due to her recognition of phenomena which had yet to be defined she drew her own conclusions. Her first study objects were deformed plants and insects, mainly Drosophila - a preferred laboratory animal of biologists. Her discovery of a special, more sensitive, bioindicator was the leaf bug, to which she was attracted initially by its beauty. She has since demonstrated that these animals have been malformed in areas contaminated by the Chernobyl accident, as well as those in the neighbourhood of other power plants. By undertaking systematic field studies in which she compared malformation rates between areas of possible contamination and areas that were considered controlled, she has proved the effects of low level radiation.

More than 60 years after American geneticist Herman J. Muller had shown that ionising radiation induces malformations, there are still many experts who represent the mainstream who will deny such effects are possible by low dose exposure of significant quantities. Cornelia Hesse-Honegger proved these effects did indeed exist within animals undergoing rapid alterations of generations, and, by extension, there is no reason to believe that similar defects will not occur in other species, all the way up to humans. She therefore exhibits a range of merits that can be associated with an independent and responsible scientist. As expected therefore, she is ignored by the "experts", or sometimes even rejected outright by means of the most threadbare "refutations". Nevertheless she remains courageous and effective, publishing her results because many responsible citizens have realised in the meantime that necessary social changes cannot be reached by placing trust in the established educational elites. It is to be hoped that the scientific work of Cornelia Hesse-Honegger will be introduced to a broader public by this publication.

Since 1973 Inge Schmitz-Feuerhake has been Professor of Experimental Physics at the University of Bremen, undertaking research on radiation dosimetry, radiation risks and health physics. In 1989 she became President of the Otto Hug Strahleninstitut, a foundation of concerned scientists. In 1990 she was a founder of the Society of Radiological Protection.

Essays

Forces of the Small: Painting as Sensuous Critique

by Peter Suchin

"We have only begun to discover the benefits of seeing science and art as one." Thomas S.Kuhn[1]

The work of Cornelia Hesse-Honegger exists at a point between conventional classifications. From the perspective of the orthodox scientific community Hesse-Honegger's paintings display, despite their obvious debt to careful observation, the subjective, and thus "unscientific" measure of the artist. In reading these pictures of wildly mutated insects as "art" orthodox science finds easy ammunition for a refutation of their implicit claim as factual records of gross disturbances within nature. The received notion of the artist proposes that such a figure is concerned not with the real but with fantasy or exaggeration. Hesse-Honegger, one speculates, must look

to be, from the purview of mainstream science, a kind of traitor to the illustrative task at hand, having supposedly abandoned the objective (and thus verifiable) recording of nature for a semi-surreal practice comprised of esoteric invention. And even when scientists accept the accuracy of the paintings their broad implications are ignored or disputed. Science wants repetition; it demands it as proof of the state of things "out there", outside and beyond individual opinion and the maverick gathering of "facts". Hesse-Honegger's paintings are, essentially, renditions of discrete creatures whose idiosyncratic deformities pose the problem of repetition and objective environmental effects in a manner science refuses to accept as meaningful. In noting the mutations of numerous single insects Hesse-Honegger's practice does point to an objectively measurable order of distortion. Even if no two creatures' deformities display a parity of genetic corruption the overall picture revealed by this research is one of widespread environmental damage. No matter that the anomalies found within individual insects don't neatly map one onto the other: such a case of multiple mutation should furnish sufficient and convincing evidence of a dangerous break within the natural pattern of nature.

But if the scientific community refuses to see these paintings as sufficiently objective, their status as art is also problematic. Hesse-Honegger trained as a scientific illustrator. Many would claim that illustration is not "art" but rather mere technique, a formulaic manner of record-making largely devoid of the innovative, critical and transformatory qualities frequently associated with artistic production (paradoxically, it is this very reading of illustration as literal and direct that should support the pictures' acceptance within the scientific field.). For one audience Hesse-Honegger's practice is invalidated by its "artistic" manner, for another it is simply not artistic enough. The pictures' execution within the ambiguous medium of watercolour further problematises their classification. Watercolour painting is not a controversial form of address. It might even be said to be a somewhat staid framework of presentation, particularly when contrasted with the various photography-based media in use today. Yet it is precisely this distance from the authority currently invested in photographic and electronic technology that gives Hesse-Honegger's pictures their critical edge. There is something slightly shocking in seeing the nightmare creatures Hesse-Honeggger depicts rendered in what Brian Eno has described as "that curious medium which seems to stand on the borderline between "Sunday painting" and "serious paintings.""[2] The format of watercolour, Eno continues:

"... does not stipulate a particular emotional range, and presents itself to a perceiver in a kind of innocent and understated way... It seems that at a time when the currency of the day is to engage in productions that are in some way epic... that which is simple and quiet suddenly becomes especially relevant."

Thus the truly disturbing implications of Hesse-Honegger's researches are most appropriately conveyed via the quiet insistence of a medium that is on the one hand at some distance from photography-related technologies and on the other is intimately bound up with painterly and illustrative traditions.

The scientific establishment normally confirms its speculative assertions through the carrying out of expensive, technically sophisticated experiments supported by high levels of both public and private funds. Those who would presume to disagree with professional science are, through their very marginality, all too easily dismissed as amateurs. There is, however, much to defend the practice of the amateur, particularly at a time when the production of knowledge is rigidly formalised within officially-sanctioned institutions. Hesse-Honegger's scientific training means that it is unreasonable to dismiss her research as that of an inexperienced "amateur", though this is precisely what professional science tries to do. Where her work does partake of the stance of the amateur is in its challenge to establishment science. "The amateur's principal purpose," suggests R. H. Stephenson, "is to...

evaluate, to the best of his ability, the results arrived at by professional practitioners."[3] The detective work involved in Hesse-Honegger's alternative assessment of scientific truth puts us in mind of that much admired if fictitious character Sherlock Holmes, whose unconventional methodologies invariably unearth a dissenting but pensive rendition of events. Holmes embodies the notion of the serious amateur, someone who refuses to take at face value the allegedly obvious. He follows his own subtle assessment of circumstance, invests not in convention but in informed observation. In "A Case of Identity" Holmes proposes: "Perhaps I have trained myself to see what others overlook," surely an approach which might well be applied to Hesse-Honegger's own vigilant investigations.[4] Holmes also observes that "It has long been an axiom of mine that the little things are infinitely the most important." Such attention to detail is also a necessary component of Hesse-Honegger's astringent research. Along with Gaston Bachelard, another perceptive critic of scientific convention, Hesse-Honegger might well propose that "the miniscule, a narrow gate, opens up an entire world."[5] If there is, intrinsically, a move towards the excessively small within Hesse-Honegger's paintings this focusing in upon the microscopic only serves to stress the immense threat posed to human and other life by nuclear power.

There are several levels of aesthetic attention or engagement within Hesse-Honegger's work. At one end of the spectrum there is that of the artist herself, magnifying through her paintings the anomalies evident in a given insect. Here the conventionally invisible is made available for inspection by the unassisted eye. The paintings themselves are small, though the insect depicted is presented many times larger than its actual size. On occasion the watercolours are further enlarged through photographic means in order to be reproduced on posters, in magazines, or in books (a means of distributing images which is in no way an anathema to Hesse-Honegger's deliberately didactic practice). This photographic enlargement offers another strata of perception and response, transmitting the painted image well beyond the narrow province of gallery-located art. Indeed it is a conventional function of the illustrator that he or she produces work with photographic reproduction in mind, the taking of an original painting being but a means to an end and not an aesthetic act in its own right.

Hesse-Honegger's paintings have been displayed both in art galleries and museums of science, being more than sufficiently complex enough to hold their own in either context, raising through their varied placing questions about the limits and alignments of "science" and of "art". The dialogue between the two supposedly opposed frameworks of science and art goes back at least several centuries, as Hesse-Honegger herself points out:

"In the fifteenth century, art was 100 years ahead of science. Nowadays, that gap has almost completely closed, but I truly believe that we cannot really see something that has not been painted or put into an artistic form. It simply does not exist until then. I believe that the artist should be incorporated into the academic world, integrated into the learning of every subject."[6]

These considerations propose a role for the artist that is not merely decorative or supplementary, but fundamental. The artist is, in this account, a figure capable of reassessing the validity of orthodox beliefs, be they scientific, religious or of any other kind. He or she is also someone who makes things visible, gives to the flux of reality a stability of meaning, isolating individual elements of the physical world in order that they be available for contemplation and critique. Criticism, in the present context, requires a move away from prevalent representations of "the real", as well as from the technologies that fix this "real" in place. The invention of photography in the nineteenth century, together with subsequent developments within and extensions of this medium was and is itself a means of producing and stabilising meanings. As Jean-Francois Lyotard has noted,

"... photographic and cinematographic processes can accomplish better, faster, and with a circulation a hundred thousand times larger than narrative or pictorial realism, the task which [nineteenth century] academicism had assigned to realism: to preserve various consciousnesses from doubt."[7]

In other words, what we take to be "the real" is not simply given or natural but is the result of a relentless, circumspect process of selection and presentation, carried out today by what Lyotard calls the "techno-sciences", those institutions and technologies responsible for the manufacture of the purportedly value-free "real". Artists such as Hesse-Honegger operate in opposition to such technologically entrenched forms of representation. Making plainly visible in her unostentatious aquarelles the structural mutations she sees through the lens of the microscope, Hesse-Honegger instigates a pause in the proceedings, bluntly disrupts the seemingly-unstoppable chain of mutually-supporting images produced by establishment science. The frozen moment of depiction given to us in these watercolours and drawings are a freeze-frame of a different order, literally allowing us a glimpse into a world the existence of which mainstream science strives to deny. Artists have often had to hold to this role as society's conscience or dissenting voice, refuting the "naturalness" of nature as conventionally defined.

It is interesting, then, that Hesse-Honegger's challenge to the authority of scientific "truth" involves the redeployment of a "pre-photographic" means of expression. Since photography still promotes itself as having an intimate and inviolable relation to the real, the "primitive" medium of painting might easily be consigned to the dustbin of out of date technologies. Why paint something when it can instead be photographed? Why utilise a subjective mode of recording when an objective means of storing information is at hand? I think a direct response to these questions is evident from a consideration of what exactly it is that Hesse-Honegger does when collecting and presenting information about the species she examines. Her pictures may be the result of numerous subjective choices but they are nonetheless true to the condition of the insect under scrutiny. Whilst it is true that Hesse-Honegger chooses to make a painting that shows the unnatural transformations in the creature's body this zooming in upon deformity is in no way a false representation. Rather, it is a means of highlighting already extant anomalies, making them directly visible (a far cry from inventing them, as she has sometimes been accused of doing). Perhaps in time the increasingly popular computer-based manipulation of photographic images will eventually make it readily evident that photography's status as a kind of unmarked mirror of the real is entirely false. Meanwhile, photography retains its place in the hierarchy of realistic devices of visual representation. Once such issues as those promulgated within Hesse-Honegger's practice are raised it is up to others to assess their validity; a task which will have to be concerned not simply with the truth of Hesse-Honegger's findings (the actual mass mutation of insects and what this implies), but with how our society constructs its picture of itself, as well as asking in whose hands the power to produce such a picture resides.

To suggest that all representations of "the real" are open to comparison and dispute is not, however, to imply that Hesse-Honegger's paintings can furnish just whatever interpretation of them a given viewer might like to make. The pictures themselves are only one part of a broader practice that includes, it must not be forgotten, the discourse around the work, including Hesse-Honegger's own public lectures and interviews, but also whatever debates are generated as a result of the existence and exhibition of the paintings. Science may deny the accuracy of Hesse-Honegger's pictures and their implications as much as it likes but, by its own standards of verification or denouncement, it must deal with them. The account of how Hesse-Honegger came to make these pictures cannot be divorced from the watercolours themselves, and any attempt to do this would be a gross misrepresentation of this practice as a whole. Implicit within this body of work and ideas is a claim for painting as a still plausible realism,

and it is ultimately to models of practice such as those employed by Courbet and the Impressionists that Hesse-Honegger's work should be connected, as opposed to, say, that of the Surrealists. This is so despite the superficially "Surreal" imagery of these paintings, because the claims being made for them are not that they show imaginary animals but real ones. When Courbet described himself as a Realist he meant by this that it was his intention to show in his paintings the world as it actually was, neither glorified nor otherwise distorted. Similarly, the Impressionists aimed at verisimilitude in their representations of everyday life and experience. The claim to truth made within Hesse-Honegger's practice is its most emphatic assertion, and the concerns she raises can readily be expressed within figurative painting, since the effects of radiation are, in the cases she records, easily visible.

"At all times," observes Theodor Adorno, "the pictorial representation of nature seems to have been authentic only when it was *nature morte*: when it had the ability to interpret nature as an encoded historical message, if not as a message of death itself."[8] Adorno's italicised term points both to "dead nature" and to "still life", and if the passage does not specifically refer to Hesse-Honegger's paintings it might nonetheless be most pertinently applied. The tragically ambiguous phrase "nature morte" seems eerily apt, as does Adorno's noting of the authentic status afforded by those works holding an encrypted historical signal or warning sign. Adorno further proposes that "The objectivity of a work of art can also be called its necessity."[9] Here too Hesse-Honegger's work might well form a most acute example, since it holds both to a directness of observation and to a point of political necessity. These two features make Adorno's comment readable at another level as well: one in which realism of expression combines with political validity in order to form an aesthetic "rightness" or formal validity.

There is, however, something slightly violent in the clash of aspects formed by the subject matter of these paintings and their precious, compact manner of execution. The subtlety and beauty of Hesse-Honegger's images contrast sharply with what they show, which is the beauty of nature, its erstwhile formal orderliness, in acute dissolution. Here, notwithstanding their accuracy of rendition, a sense of the Surreal does creep in, as though we are looking at creatures out of Lautréamont or Jules Verne. André Breton's stipulation that "Beauty will be CONVULSIVE or it will not be at all" is a sentence in which one can now uncover (in the light of Hesse-Honegger's pictures) an entirely other strand of understanding.[10] Painting beautiful watercolours of grotesquely deformed insects has, in itself, a certain monstrosity, conceptually so if not necessarily at the level of the retinal. Poussin's famous painting showing "The Arcadian Shepherds" finding proof of corruption at the heart of what had appeared to be a paradise on earth is another image to which Hesse-Honegger's work can be compared, for both artists show that within the quiet, everyday order of things there may well lurk a darker force, its very presence implying total desolation. (11)

Figurative painting is, finally, an odd medium in which to depict something that is in fact invisible: the radiation leaked from nuclear power stations. In order to record the deleterious consequences of this strange spectral energy Hesse-Honegger has followed a line of thought expressed by a renowned poet whose work one would hardly think to connect with her own. "Paint," wrote Mallarmé in 1864, "not the thing, but the effect it produces." (12) These words describe, perfectly if inadvertently, Cornelia Hesse-Honegger's critical and artistic project.

Peter Suchin is a critic, painter and teacher whose writings have appeared in a variety of journals including Art Monthly, Artists Newsletter, Circa, Variant, Mute, Here and Now and Contemporary Art. His paintings are discussed in Paul Crowther, Critical Aesthetics and Postmodernism, Oxford University Press, 1993.

1   Thomas S. Kuhn, *The Essential Tension*, University of Chicago Press, 1977, p. 343.
2   This and the following quotation, Brian Eno, "Peter Schmidt and Brian Eno", *Arts Review*, Vol. XXIX, No. 25, 9 December, 1977, p. 737.
3   R. H. Stephenson, "Last Universal Man - or Wilful Amateur?", in Elizabeth M. Wilkinson (Ed.), *Goethe Revisited*, John Calder, 1984, p. 56. For further discussion of the amateur see Peter Suchin, "The Destruction of Art as an Institution: The Role of the Amateur", *Variant*, No. 5, Summer/Autumn 1988.
4   This and the following quotation, Arthur Conan Doyle, quoted in Michael and Mollie Hardwick, *The Sherlock Holmes Companion*, John Murray, 1962, p. 154. Naomi Schor has strongly suggested that attention to detail in artistic matters is an attribute closely connected with "the feminine". See her *Reading in Detail: Aesthetics and the Feminine*, Methuen, 1987, and the review of this work by Peter Suchin, *The British Journal of Aesthetics*, Vol. 28, No. 4, Autumn 1988.
5   Gaston Bachelard, *The Poetics of Space*, Beacon Press, 1969, p. 155.
6   Cornelia Hesse-Honegger, quoted in Jeremy Hall, "A terrible beauty", *The Independent Magazine*, 30 March, 1996, p. 11. An obvious example of a Renaissance figure operating across categories that only later became rigidly demarcated is that of Leonardo da Vinci.
7   Jean-François Lyotard, *The Postmodern Condition*, Manchester University Press, 1984, p. 74. See also Lyotard's "Presenting the Unpresentable: The Sublime", *Artforum*, April 1982.
8   T. W. Adorno, *Aesthetic Theory*, R.K.P., 1984, p. 100.
9   Adorno, op. cit., p. 114.
10 André Breton, *Nadja*, Grove Press, 1960, p. 160.
11 On this work by Poussin see Erwin Panofsky, "*Et in Arcadia Ego*: Poussin and the Elegiac Tradition", in Panofsky, *Meaning in the Visual Arts*, Penguin, 1970.
12 Stéphane Mallarmé, quoted in Anthony Hartley, "Introduction", in Hartley (Ed.) *Mallarmé*, Penguin, 1970, p. ix (translation modified).

The work of Cornelia Hesse-Honegger - a scientist's perspective

by Georges B. Dussart

For a millennium, biologists have used drawings and paintings as a means of summarising and recording their observations. A drawing integrates eye, hand and mind in a way which is difficult to achieve with a camera and in a single illustration; many intricate views can be expressed. Cornelia Hesse-Honegger has, by her exquisitely produced drawings of insects, shown herself to be an accomplished exponent of this long standing tradition. The technical expertise is breathtaking, even when measured alongside other great biological illustrators. However, her choice of her subjects for these elegant drawings raises eyebrows and questions. The drawings show malformed insects which have been found near nuclear installations and, in the context of the damage which ionising radiations can do, it is easy to make a causative relationship between developmental damage (teratogeny) and nuclear radiation.

The really interesting question about her work is 'Is it art or science?' For example, Audubon's work was done with the talent of an artist but with the intentions of a scientist, and this marriage charged his work with something which a 'plain' piece of art or science might not have otherwise had. Hesse-Honegger is in the same class, except that, in addition, she has a powerful message which she wants put across.

Throughout the story of the development of biology, there has been a gradual shift in emphasis from description to explanation, and it is the predictive element, arising from explanation, which makes biology into a science. Prediction is one of the essential parts of the definition of a science. In this context, only predictions which work are valid, and there is an implication of repeatability in the use of the word 'work'. For example, I could probably use magic, such as casting runes, to predict where a lightning bolt might strike the earth but it is unlikely that I would be repeatedly successful in making predictions by such a method. On the other hand, I could use an elementary knowledge of science from the time of Benjamin Franklin to predict that lightning will tend to strike tall, wet objects. I could then try to see whether this prediction is true or not.

Without falling into the morass of metaphysical argument, it is in the nature of scientists to believe that there is an objective reality, and that this reality is discoverable. To a scientist, a spherical earth represents a more real entity than a flat earth. Discovering, describing and predicting from this objective reality is the everyday job of the everyday scientist. Unfortunately, as for humans in many other contexts, the scientist must be sensitive to the problems posed by the self-fulfilling prophecy. The good scientist achieves this by being scrupulously honest. At the start of a test, the good scientist adopts the position of trying to prove that the prediction does not work. In other words, the scientist says, I think A causes B but then adopts a mind-set, and experimental protocol, which tries to show that A and B are not related. Technically, this is called a null-hypothesis and the scientist concludes by accepting or refuting the null hypothesis. By this means, the scientist hopes to avoid bringing too much personal bias to the exploratory adventure.

The science of ionising radiation is an area in which an objective view of reality has been particularly difficult to obtain and the reasons probably cut very deep. Firstly, the scientific study of ionising radiation is young, dating only from the turn of the century. Its development coincides with technological developments which mean both an increased reliance on, and trust in, technology in our daily lives. Secondly, by use of such technologies as those involved in the media and the administration of bureaucracy, governments command greater legitimacy and power. In the first part of the twentieth century people tended to trust their leaders, and were led into two world wars as a consequence. Their trust partly derived from the propaganda which was made possible through technology. For example, it became a matter of national pride to explode a larger test atom bomb than the competition, or to develop the newest nuclear reactor. Little thought was given to effects of ionising radiation, and no thought was given to disposal of the waste. The people trusted their elected representative to do the right thing on their behalf and there is increasing evidence to show that their trust was misplaced.

So what are the effects of ionising radiations? The blood and immune systems are most sensitive. Once the immune system is damaged by radiation, the symptoms are very similar to those shown by an AIDS victim. With a higher dose, the alimentary canal (gut) becomes affected and with even higher doses, the central nervous system (brain and sense organs) are affected. Depending on the dose received, blood and immune system damage can be survived, but the more serious gut and nervous system damage can be horribly fatal. Radiation damage at this kind of level will almost certainly cause quite serious burns.

If the radiation is received by an organism which is still growing, the organism can show deformities as it grows and develops. For example, radiation received by a foetus in the human womb can result in babies being born with no back to the head. In these cases of deformity (teratogeny), there has almost certainly been some damage to the DNA in the cells. The DNA contains the genes. These are a set of instructions which allow the cell to function correctly. The DNA is also the blueprint for the eventual role of the cell and if this blueprint is damaged, the cell will not develop properly to fulfill its role in a co-ordinated, whole organism.

So far, the description has been relevant to the cells which make up the main body of the organism - the soma. This is the part we see - the part which grows, develops, moves, respires etc. However, there is another part which we don't usually see. This is the part which contributes to the development of the next generation - the gonads and sex cells. These cells, which contain the genes for the next generation, appear to be susceptible to low doses of radiation. If a damaged gene from a sperm ends up paired with a similarly damaged gene from an egg, the corresponding foetus may be deformed and would almost certainly die. A damaged gene is a mutated gene, and, as shown by Muller in 1927, gene mutations are almost always lethal. Often, mutated genes will directly or indirectly cause cancer. However, Cornelia Hesse-Honegger has illustrated relatively successful mutations, since the organism has survived long enough to be documented, thereby alerting us to the possibility of a serious environmental problem.

An interesting ramification of the way the genes work in higher organisms such as humans is that there are pairs of dominant and recessive genes. Dominant genes are always expressed and show themselves in characters of the organism. However, recessive genes are not expressed if there is a partner gene which is dominant. This means that a recessive gene could pass through millions of generations without being expressed, until it meets with an appropriate partner recessive gene. If such a recessive gene had mutated during its hidden history, the lethal effects would not come to light until it became expressed. Any human being carries millions of recessive genes and probably thousands of these have been mutated through quite natural events. However, repeated exposure of the human population to mutagens such as ionising radiations or mutagenic chemicals could mean that we are building up a hidden bank of mutated recessive genes which might be expressed, when they achieve a sufficient density, several generations hence.

Because the effects of ionising radiation are hidden, the general public has had to rely on government agencies to define levels of risk. Governments invested heavily in these agencies, partly through the military-industrial-nuclear (MIN) complex, and nuclear processors developed their own enormous financial and administrative momentum. It therefore benefited the MIN complex to underestimate and under-report risks and events and even to falsify documents. The Windscale fire is an example of the former, and the Salter Duck debacle is an example of the latter. As more of these anomalies came to light, the general public became much more doubting and cynical about the role of its elected representatives and the value of nuclear power. Chernobyl may have sounded its death knell.

This gloomy picture is, to some extent, mitigated by the fact that it now appears that cells have sophisticated systems for recognising and repairing damage to DNA. Indeed, it is the biotechnological use of these systems which underpins the current significant advances in genetic engineering.

So, Hesse-Honegger's illustrations make a strong case for a particular viewpoint. Reading her text reinforces the anxiety engendered by seeing the paintings themselves. Looking through her account I can see two things. Firstly, a heartfelt anxiety about the state of affairs in relation to radioactive contamination. This manifests itself in a thorough, descriptive approach to looking at insects in relation to nuclear plants or accidents. Secondly, a commendable investigation into the background and history of these nuclear plants.

From an artistic point of view, there is a case for saying there is a role for art in being subversive. In challenging the dogmas of the MIN-Government complex, Hesse-Honegger is being both subversive and evangelical. Unfortunately, evangelists often get accused of heresy by the high priests of orthodoxy. Hesse-Honegger's own account seems to indicate that this has happened to her.

Since Plato wrote the dialogues of Socrates and Meno, we have used dialectical argument to push knowledge on. It has to be accepted that certain people, as is their right, disagree with Hesse-Honegger's viewpoint. She herself catalogues these disagreements in her description of the development of her work.

As such, she is faced with two possible strategies when dealing with the mainstream scientific community. She can accept that as an evangelist she will always run the risk of being labelled a heretic, or she can tackle the High Priests of Science on their own ground and challenge them to abandon the null-hypothesis; in this case the null-hypothesis is that there is no effect of ionising radiations, and that the incidence rate of malformations is approximately the same everywhere. If this can be refuted then something else must be true (i.e. that there are identifiable clusters of malformations).

To some extent Hesse-Honegger has already shown this. Her Lake District investigations seem to show much lower incidence rates of malformations. She has plotted the results on maps showing that the incidence rates increase as you get closer to the plants. From a scientific viewpoint, Hesse-Honegger's illustrations raise questions which require answers and therefore, as well as being artistically delightful, have a high scientific value in themselves. The illustrations constitute the genesis of a hypothesis; executed with a scientific eye for detail but, at the same time, endeavouring to make a sociological case.

In my opinion the workings of the nuclear industry raise serious questions for society. I admire Hesse-Honegger for acting as an evangelist in this context; the fact that her work creates such ire in the scientific community makes it exciting. It is not only a record of circumstances which have been inadequately explained or poorly investigated by the scientific community, but it is also a body of artistic work with a chilling message.

Georges B. Dussart is a Franco-English scientist who teaches, and researches, ecology and ionising radiation biology on the 'Degree Programme in Natural and Environmental Sciences' at Canterbury Christ Church University College.

Preface

by Cornelia Hesse-Honegger

As a scientific illustrator specialising in zoology I had my professional training at the University of Zürich, in the Department of Zoology. My main task was to illustrate scientific publications on taxonomy, and laboratory-induced mutations of the fly family Drosophilidae. The mutations were created in the laboratory by putting a mutagene poison into the flies' food. In 1965 I had to draw the mutated lab flies for a publication, and became so taken with this task that I also started to paint them in my free time in aquarelle paint. I later realised that a similar poison to the one that was used in the University of Zürich - 'Agent Orange' - was used during the war in Vietnam by the US Army to get rid of the foliage in the jungle (thereby making it easier to detect the Vietcong from the air). In Vietnam today a misshapen child is born every day. I cannot recall whether the geneticists working worldwide with mutated Drosophila, who knew about the mutagenic effects of Agent Orange, were alarmed, or had protested openly. I have heard no apology issued so far by the United States for its use (in contrast to President Clinton's apology to the victims of the radiobiological experiments conducted in the United States between 1940 and the early seventies).

Later, when I lived in the countryside and had children of my own to care, for I worked less for zoologists, but increasingly drew and painted the insects I found living around my house in Gockhausen, near Zürich. At this time, in 1971, I developed a preference for the leaf bugs (Heteroptera) because of their beautiful patterns and colours. About 600 different species can be found in Switzerland. They have a length of between 2mm and 2cm. The larva slips out of the egg as a tiny animal. They live by sucking the liquid out of plants, and change their skin approximately five times until reaching adulthood (a stage known as *imago*). They live on specific plants over generations; it is easy to find them on the same plant every summer.

At the end of the seventies and the beginning of the eighties I began to worry about some species which hadn't shown up for several summers. As I did not use any poisons in the garden, and only cut the grass once a year in the autumn, my worries increased; it became obvious to me that something else must be restricting their lives. I worried that these species were vanishing without any recognition of the problem. I tried to find people who might be interested in my concerns, even going as far as suggesting to a professor in the Zoological Department in Zürich that someone should find out which species were still actually alive. Today, I can say that many of them are now lost, as I cannot find them in the locations where I had once been able to find them every summer over so many years.

I didn't want to contribute to the deaths of the leaf

bugs by my own inaction, so I started to paint flies that I found in great varieties around my own house. In these aquarelles I started to create pictures with simple random programmes. For example, I would paint the thorax of flies in series, based on the order in which I found them.

I thought perhaps that I was clinging to an idealised concept of nature that had nothing to do with what is actually around us. What, I asked myself, does reality really look like? Mutated laboratory flies, I imagined, are perhaps closer to today's reality of nature or, maybe, are prototypes for a future aesthetics of nature.

In 1985 I asked a professor of genetics at the University of Zürich to give me mutated flies from the laboratory to paint. At the time I learnt that the flies were no longer mutated by poison; rather, the new technique was to irradiate them with x-rays.

Whilst I was in the process of painting a mutated housefly - with legs growing out of its feelers, curved wings, yellow eyes and body - the Chernobyl disaster happened.

For me it was a given fact that the fallout from Chernobyl had contaminated a wide area. I imagined that it had effectively changed nature into a laboratory situation; and that within this context I would find deformed leaf bugs. The professor who mutated the flies with x-rays was a nice man, and it seemed to me at first that he did not want me to be frightened. I later came to understand, however, that he was convinced that the low radiation that fell along the cloud trail - of doses below those found in natural radiation or below the level used in x-rays for research - could not cause any harm, let alone visible bodily deformations.

In spite of such reassurances I travelled to Sweden in the summer of 1987, to the area that had received the heaviest fallout of all of western Europe. I had waited a year for the next generation of insect to grow since the fallout from 1986. The different colours and forms of plant life, and the visible deformations on leaf bugs that I observed there did indeed confirm my fears that the fallout from Chernobyl had changed the appearance of nature.

Once back home I travelled to Ticino, the area that in May 1986 had received the heaviest fallout in Switzerland. The vegetation in the south is more abundant at the beginning of May than in Sweden (where the snow lies longer and the nights are longer), resulting in an earlier development of vegetation and insects. In May, at the time of the fallout, the leaf bug larvae were therefore already on the leaves, sucking liquid (whereas in Sweden the eggs were probably not even laid yet; the adults leaf bugs still hidden in earth or below leaves waiting for spring). Even though the dose was 'only' a quarter of that received by Sweden I thought that the effects would be similar, as the larvae were exposed to direct radiation from the cloud and, in addition, it was raining heavily (later comparison supported this, in that the types of deformities that I found in insects from both areas were the same).

Studying the bugs more closely I got the idea to collect Drosophilidae for breeding purposes. I collected them in Rancate, Ticino, taking three pairs home. I started to breed them in my kitchen, using the same kind of food as the University used. Looking at the hundreds of Drosophila melanogaster flies from the parents caught at Ticino (two of the parents did not produce offspring), I detected terrible deformations on their bodies when viewed through the microscope. It seemed essential to me to publish the results of my work, which I did in the magazine Tages-Anzeiger in January 1988.[1] I wrote a text explaining my theory that these morphological deformations were induced by the fallout from Chernobyl, which was supported by aquarelles of the deformed leaf bugs from Sweden, Ticino, and the Drosophila flies.

Neither I nor anybody else had made a similar study before this time; it was my idea to collect the leaf bugs and study them. I knew nothing about radioactivity and its effects. Neither had I previously made a study of the impact of such a phenomenon on nature. Nevertheless, the resultant criticism and anger that came from the scientific community indicated to me that I had hit a vulnerable spot. I, by comparison, could not understand why nothing had been done, or was being done, to try and understand what was going on in a natural world subjected to such terrible conditions.

The International Commission for Radiological Protection (ICRP) decided that a worker in the atomic industry should accumulate no more than 5 rem (rem is an acronym for *roentgen equivalent man*, a unit of radiation dosage received which has the equivalent effect as one rad, a unit of radiation) in 30 years; a total considered harmless by the ICRP, but one which I would contest.[2] The subsequent conclusion drawn from this is that anybody who has been irradiated with a smaller amount and feels ill is considered to feel so due to their fear of radiation; they are, in short, considered to be suffering from radiophobia. Even when the Chernobyl accident had occurred the experts were convinced that no harm could be predicted for the future; such thinking was most prevalent in western Europe and the United States.

This reaction failed to convince me, though; the only way to learn more about these problems was to continue with my studies in the environs of Swiss nuclear power plants in the knowledge that they constantly emit low level radiation both day and night. If the bugs that I found here were healthy than I would be proven wrong, and consequently there would have to be other reasons for the deformities I found in Sweden and Ticino.

In 1988 I began to walk in the main wind directions of the power plants Gösgen and Leibstadt, collecting bugs at several spots. The deformities that I found shocked me deeply. The publication of a text and aquarelles by me detailing my findings in early 1989[3] resulted in a seemingly endless debate about the effects of low radiation, and the harmfulness of nuclear power plants in general. After the publication of this article the anger of Swiss scientists increased. They accused me of frightening innocent people with lies that had no basis in scientific evidence.

In the summer of 1989 I travelled to Sellafield BNFL in Great Britain to examine the health of bugs in the neighbourhood of the plant (which had an extremely bad reputation). I already knew that Switzerland exported its own nuclear waste to Sellafield for reprocessing, and in my eyes the Swiss were also responsible for what was happening there. The worst damage that I found on bugs and leaf hoppers was in Seascale, Drigg, Ponsonby and near the plant itself.

In the summer of 1990 I was invited to travel with a group of parliamentarians and journalists in order to more closely view the effects of the Chernobyl disaster. The group 'Strom Ohne Atom' ('Energy Without Atoms') - which had the aim of closing down all the nuclear power plants in Switzerland - wanted to give these invited people the chance to see how the results of a similar accident would appear in Switzerland. I was able to join the group, which gave me the opportunity to study the nature there and collect leaf bugs (so that, later on, I would be able to compare them to others that I had found near Swiss power plants and in Sellafield).

The activities of this group eventually resulted in the establishment in 1990 of an 'Initiative'; in which a national Swiss vote is made via solicited signatures. Whilst the group proposed radical new energy laws - including a complete ban on nuclear power plants, and the exclusive use of renewable energy sources - the public voted for the less radical proposal of the package: a ten year moratorium on the construction of any new nuclear power plants. Nevertheless, this in itself was a victory. I was happy to support the Initiative, even though it had nothing to do with my own work.

The group went to several places in and around Chernobyl, in order to look at the effects of such a catastrophe and how an area could survive. During this time I collected as many bugs as possible. Seeing the suffering that people there were experiencing made me extremely sad. It was obvious that the basic human right to a healthy life was non-existent. At the time 600,000 soldiers and workers - known as 'liquidators' - were working within Chernobyl's 30km exclusion zone, cleaning up the mess. Coming from different regions of the Soviet Union, many were exposed to radiation over an average of two months, often without proper safety equipment or radiation badges. How was it possible to expose healthy young men to heavy radiation without telling them what risks they were taking? How was it possible to tell people they were only suffering from radiophobia - and not of radiation-induced illnesses - without really studying their illnesses and taking them seriously? Why are humans so cruel?

In 1991 I travelled to the Three Mile Island nuclear power plant in Pennsylvania USA, the site of an accidental radioactive leak on March 28 1979. I was interested in studying the leaf bugs situated within the main wind directions, and to ascertain if there had been a definite morphological change since the accident had taken place. Fortunately I only found misshapen bugs and leaf hoppers in the areas that closely surrounded the plant, which might hopefully mean that the effects in nature of such accidents may disappear with time.

In 1992 the Swiss Federal Office of Culture presented an exhibition and accompanying book of my work called 'After Chernobyl', which was used to represent the Swiss contribution at the XVIII Triennial in Milan. This exhibition subsequently toured to several places in Switzerland, Vienna and Sweden, as well as to venues in Newcastle upon Tyne and Oxford in 1996, and (with an additional exhibition called "The Future's Mirror") to Leeds, Middlesbrough and Nottingham in 1997. Both exhibitions will be shown in Vancouver in the autumn of 1998.

As I had requested in the article published in 1989, a scientific study on the health of leaf bugs in Switzerland was instigated at the Federal Institute of Technology ETH (Eidgenössische Technische Hochschule - the Swiss equivalent of a national technical university) by a zoologist called Dr. J. Jenny.[4] He collected 10,000 fire bugs (Pyrrhocoris apterus) and other species, and gave me (at my request) misshapen bugs to paint. After a period of time I came to realise that he was suppressing information that some of the worst deformed leafbugs were found in the Canton of Aargau, within the area of the Paul Scherrer Institute itself. In addition he did not name the places where the bugs had been searched for, nor indicate which malformations he had found where. I consequently considered his work to be unreliable, and did not continue with the collaboration. One article by him published in the monthly university paper showed me that he was not prepared to make any awkward or controversial statements in an official scientific context. His paper was maliciously interpreted by the press to show that my work was without any scientific value.

Some of the worst deformations that the zoologist did give me came from the interior area of the Paul Scherrer Institute, where nuclear research was being undertaken with a still working (at the time) integrated reactor. Whilst the zoologist was allowed to search inside I did not benefit from having any official status and it was not possible for me to do likewise. Forbidden to collect specimens inside I decided to collect bugs from the outside of the institute. During the summers of 1992 up to 1997 I collected bugs from the same spot. The damage that I observed was always of up to 15% of the population. I also decided to make a more systematic study of the health of bugs, not throughout the whole of Switzerland but concentrating on the Cantons of Aargau and Solothurn, where four of the Swiss power plants are located. Using the official coordination points on the map, at a distance of 10 km from point to point, I searched for 65 bugs at a time at 15 separate points. In order to obtain a random selection of 25 spots within these squares I threw a dice. I then looked for the comparable number (65) of bugs per spot. For the first time I was able to show where, and which kind of, deformations could be found on maps. I found the highest rate of morphological disturbances (not just in terms of quantity but also in terms of severity of deformity) - 15% - in Rohr, an area situated approximately 5 km NE from Gösgen. Second highest was Rüfenach, S of Leibstadt, Beznau and the Paul Scherrer Institute, with 14%. Third was Kleindöttingen, SE of Leibstadt, with 11%. The wind there blows south-north and north-south. The closer one came to the Canton of Zürich in the east, the less leaf bugs are damaged: 0% in Othmarsingen. It is interesting to see in the area surrounding the Gösgen power plant - which is supposed to be the cleanest plant in the whole of Switzerland - that the largest number of bugs and with the heaviest deformations were found. This was already evident from the first study that I made there in 1988, as well as the latest during the period 1993 to 1996.

When I look at the deformations on feelers I see that those feelers with one section missing were found in Rohr, Kleindöttingen and Auw. Wings of uneven lengths I found in Möhlin, Rohr, Kleindöttingen and Döttingen. Scientists believe that mutations are a normal occurrence and that every now and then one can be found in nature, due to factors such as difficult weather or heat.

Whenever I was asked about my work by academically educated people or scientists, the first question put to me was always whether I had used a biotope for reference. A biotope is a natural place with a specific formation of plants and animals supporting its own distinctive community, such as a forest or the border of a lake. It is used for comparison with the area being examined, in order to chart any discrepancies between the two. My own reference biotope is in the Swiss Alps, where there are no nuclear power plants.

I don't, however, exactly believe that the use of a reference biotope is necessary. It is hard to agree with the academic and scientific notion of an unspoilt 'paradisical' location; as there is so much undetected pollution, say from bomb tests or Chernobyl. It is difficult to say whether a biotope is really healthy or not without carrying out chemical studies (what I can say, at least, is that when I went to the Swiss and Italian Alps the bugs I found looked healthy and fine). As I don't believe in paradise, I studied 40 different spots in the Canton of Aargau (which indicate that the results become worse as one approaches the power plants).

During this period of work I began to differentiate morphological disturbances from changes in pigment, or from dark patches on the chitin armour.

Danger of Radioactivity in Low Doses

Low radiation seems to be a topic that has been neglected since 1939, when Prof. and Nobel Prize winner Herman J. Muller made his research on x-ray induced mutations on Drosophila.

Knowledge based on the development of nuclear weapons was later used for the production of nuclear energy. This seems to be one reason why information about the effects of man made radioactivity has been kept secret (the bomb tests and experiments overseen by universities were commissioned by the military, and the results are therefore subject to various secrecy acts). Almost no literature can be found concerning the effects of what is called low level radiation. Official science tries to make us believe that artificial radiation in low doses, below the level of natural radiation, is equally harmless.

Studies made in laboratories of Drosophila larvae that had been exposed to x-rays at 2,500 rem and more show mutations. In order to put the strength of this dosage into perspective, remember that it had been decreed that a worker in the atomic industry should accumulate no more than 5 rem in a 30 year period. If the radiation is lessened the insects show no damage. Scientists extrapolate from these studies on the effects of low radiation and effectively attempt to propose that low radiation from Chernobyl or from around other power plants is therefore harmless. This ignores the fact that laboratory flies are irradiated with external radiation, whereas people or animals in contaminated regions are exposed to radiation mainly through the food chain i.e. through contact with air, water and food. I ask myself how it is possible for them to come to such conclusions, knowing that incorporated radionuclides - such as Caesium-137, Plutonium or Iodine-131 - can have a different effect than x-rays on living cells. Why is there no distinction being made between internal and external exposure, or between gamma, beta and alpha rays?

In analysing the effects of radiation exposure, mainstream scientists consider the dose-response relationship as linear: that is, the lower the dose the less significant the effect on the living cell. Yet since 1972 research by Dr. A. Petkau has proposed a supralinear dose-response relationship: that is, the more the dosage approaches zero the greater the possible effect. Petkau argues, in addition, that radiation damages the large surface of a cell - not only the small cell nucleus, as was previously thought. This indirect damage to the cell membrane manifests itself strongly at lower doses, leading to a concave downwards dose-effect curve, which climbs more rapidly in the lower dose range than the linear model that scientists accept as a given.[5]

For example, Prof. R. K. Whyte, of MacMaster University in Hamilton, California, reports that official governmental weapons tests during the 1950s and 60s had caused in excess of 320,000 infant deaths in the United States of America and Great Britain by 1980. He attempted to explain that even though the radiation dose from weapons tests was less high than that of exposure from natural radiation its effects are nevertheless worse. As Petkau maintained, low doses of artificial radioactivity have a greater effect than those higher doses over and above the natural threshold.[6]

Dr. Ivan Bubriak, of the Academy of Science in Kiev presented a lecture at the Paul Scherrer Institute in November 1991, stating that one of the most important tasks for radioecologists is "to estimate the genetic risk to plant populations growing under different levels of radionuclide contamination. One convenient method to estimate such effects is to investigate chromosome aberration frequencies using radiosensitive generative cells, such as barley pollen. The mutagenic effectiveness of chronic mixed alpha- beta- and gamma-radiation from Chernobyl fallout was compared to gamma-irradiation from an external cobalt-60 source. Lower dose rates were more effective in producing mutations than higher dose rates, and greater genotoxicity was observed from mixed-irradiation than from the gamma-irradiation. It seems that mutagenic effect in plant cells do not depend entirely on the total dose, but also on specific radionuclide mixture and possible toxi-chemical synergism".[7]

I think the time has come for the official world of science to acknowledge the dangers of low, artificial radiation. I am very concerned that current cell mutations indicate that the entire hereditary process, in both humans and nature, is being disturbed in wide areas of the world without our even knowing it. The generations that are alive now will not be the ones to suffer the most; but thegenerations that follow will. When we are dead this next generation may realise the disaster that we have provoked.

Artists and scientists need to work together in new forms of research, and the conclusions of this interdisciplinary research should be made publicly available in order to find new solutions to our problems. The difference between 1987 and now is that at least the effects of low radiation are being discussed, and many scientists are surprised by what they are finding. I am convinced that artificial radioactivity in low doses is dangerous. If the only way to stop the daily disaster is to frighten people, than I am happy if my paintings help.

Field Study made in the Canton of Aargau
and the Canton of Solothurn 1993 - 1996

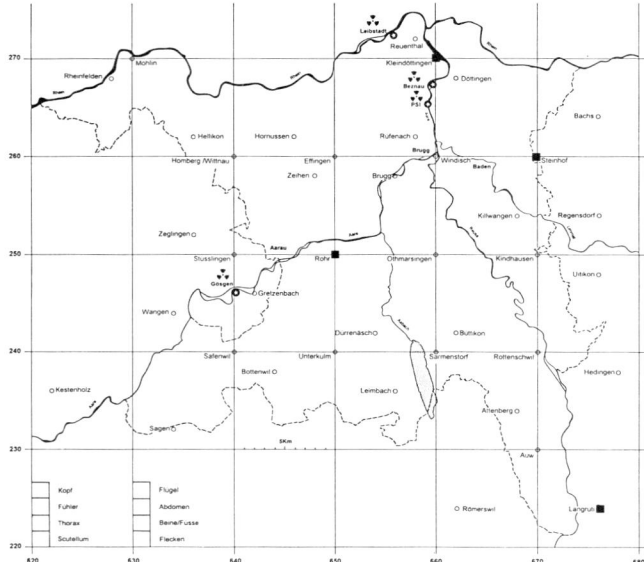

Each black square indicates where I found insects with asymmetric deformations of the thorax.

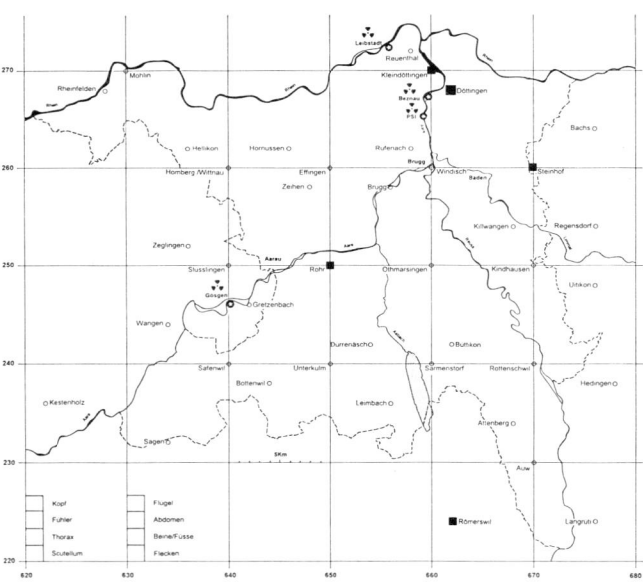

Each black square indicates where I found insects with deformations of uneven wings.

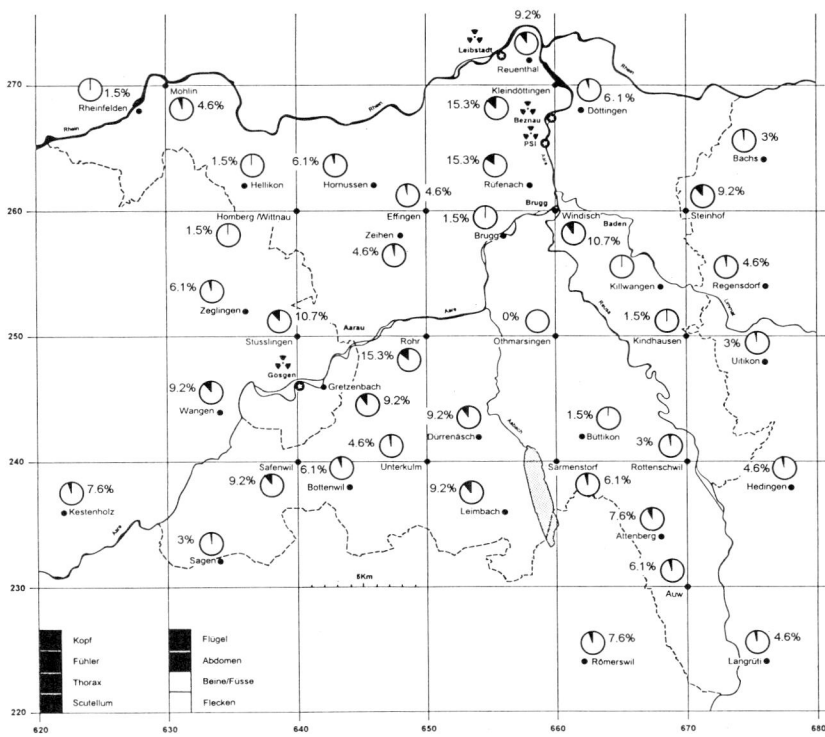

Morphological deformations listed as percentage of 65 leaf bugs found in each site. The sites where the leaf bugs were collected were determined by fixed and random systems.

Fixed point system:

Möhlin	Kindhausen
Kleindöttingen	Safenwil
Homberg/Wittnau	Unterkulm
Effingen	Sarmenstorf
Windisch	Rottenschwil
Rohr	Auw
Othamrsingen	Steinhof
Stüsslingen	

Random system:

Reuenthal	Killwangen
Hornussen	Durrenäsch
Rüfenach	Büttikon
Döttingen	Bottenwil
Zeihen	Ättenberg
Brugg	Gretzenbach
Langrüti	Wangen
Römerswil	Uitikon
Rheinfelden	Kestenholz
Hellikon	Sagen
Bachs	Leimbach
Zeglingen	Hedingen
Regensdorf	

Sweden

After the accident at Chernobyl in 1986 I decided to go to Sweden, where the worst fallout from Chernobyl had hit western Europe.

I started to study maps showing the trajectory of the clouds over Europe, and tried to become acquainted with the meaning of terms such as Becquerel (Bq), rem, Sievert (Sv) and radioactivity in general. I had never thoughts about such matters before. I tried to calculate a whole body dose for a leaf bug larva - which measures less than a millimeter when it first slips out of its egg. I was convinced that leaf bugs would be good indicators of any change in body shape, since they suck the liquid out of leaves from the first moment that they come out of the egg. They change their skin five times before reaching adulthood, during which growth can be endangered. As it was possible to predict that misshapen leaf bugs would not be seen until the next generation it was necessary, therefore, to wait for the summer of 1987.

On maps printed in November 1986 by the Swiss Division of the Security of Nuclear Installations, Ministry of Energy, one can easily detect that the radioactive cloud that emanated from Chernobyl did not stop on the border of the 30 km exclusion zone surrounding the plant! Before reaching Moscow it was 'shot down' (by decision of the Soviet government); as a consequence 70% of the fallout from Chernobyl contaminated Belarus, in particular the area around the city of Gomel.[1] Today families there have 30% (11/1000) less children compared to 1985, because they are afraid to have ill or deformed babies.[2]

The cloud had also moved over Poland and the Baltic countries. On April 27 and 28 a high pressure area over Russia drifted east, as a low pressure zone went up north. It caused rainfall over Germany and parts of Scandinavia.

On the morning of April 28 at 7:00, the cloud drifted for the second time over Sweden and was detected by the power plant at Forsmark. 53 hours after the accident radioactivity was noticed for the first time. The radioactivity was 10-150 times higher than normal, and Sweden was afraid that one of its own power plants had had a leakage. A few hours later 16 different types of radionuclides were detected. Ruthenium was found, which melts at a temperature of 2250°C (Isotope 103 and 106) and this was taken as proof that a meltdown had happened somewhere. Jod-131, Caesium-134, Caesium-137 and Tellur-132 were also found as well. Information about the wind direction was analysed, and the fact that a serious accident in the Soviet Union had occurred was quickly diagnosed. The Soviet government was forced to confess the catastrophe, and western governments were informed officially on the same day.

On April 28 and 29 1986, it rained in Gävle and the surrounding area. In the territory of Gävle 140,000 Bq/m2 was measured, and even later in May 1986 200,000 Bq/m2 was measured - an amount 80 times higher than from all the atomic bomb tests since 1945. It was forbidden to eat vegetables, mushrooms or berries, and to drink milk in heavily contaminated areas such as Gävleborg. In areas such as Västernorrland fish were recorded as having 5,040 Bq/kg. On June 1987 the threshold for selling contaminated meat and fish was raised from 300 to 1,500 Bq/kg. Also, the Lapp population was severely hit: 50,000 reindeer had to be killed when 4,000 Bq/kg was measured in the meat.[3]

I arrived in Uppsala on July 21 1987. In my luggage was the microscope, paper, aquarelle paint, pencils and everything that I needed to start painting bugs, as well as the equipment to catch them.

After installing my studio in a wonderful hotel in Gysinge I had the chance to meet some friendly and helpful people. Some were teachers from Österfärnebo, a town near the hotel, where the heaviest fallout was measured in the school yard. Two teachers from the school told me that they woke up during the night of April 29, when it was raining heavily. From their accounts it seemed that their bodies had sensed something that the mind could not read. A veterinarian showed me a clover plant which had dark red leaves, and yellow flowers instead of pink. He also mentioned that an unusual amount of deformed calves had been born that summer. An elderly lady told me that 1,000 Bq/m2 had been measured in her garden in the summer of 1986, and that many people didn't like to eat any of their own plants. Even in the summer of the following year people had not really enjoyed planting anything, because they were not sure how healthy the vegetables were.

My new friends were curious about the reasons for my stay in this region, and I explained that I was looking to see if leaf bugs were morphologically affected by the Chernobyl fallout.

On July 27 I went to the school at Österfärnebo, where 380-400 Micro Röntgen/h (radiation waves per hour) had been measured on May 5 in 1986. It was empty due to the summer holidays. I imagined children playing in the sandboxes, where the sand had not even been changed. Since it was raining that day I only found a few bugs, so I therefore collected leaves from the trees, which looked heavily deformed. I noticed many dark red plants as well. Looking at the bugs with the microscope, a larva of the family Miridae had a heavy deformation on the left wings.

On July 30 I went to Gävle where, on May 5 1986, 100 Micro Röntgen/h had been measured. Even though it was cold and raining, I collected leaves and some bugs. One soft bug had a deformed foot, and the leaves were heavily misshapen.

In Gysinge, where, on May 5 1986, 150-200 Micro Röntgen/h had been measured, I found bugs with deformations on the feelers that looked like sausages, and a growth out of one eye. I started to draw and paint from morning until night. During my sleep I was persecuted by nightmares, convinced I had found a terrible truth in spite of the appeasing talk of the scientists. It became evident to me that deformations were not only linked to high but also to lower - and even the lowest - radiation, contrary to today's scientific theories. The disturbed bugs I had found around the hotel were as much and as often disturbed as the ones from Gävle or Österfärnebo, even though the biotopes there were more natural than in the towns. I felt it was necessary to empty my mind of all that I knew scientifically, and to open it to new, and possibly terrifying, realities and associations. I was confused. I believed I had become mad, doing such work without being qualified. I convinced myself that somewhere in Sweden scientists were doing just this kind of work. I tried to get in contact with biologists, helped by a new friend who worked in the hotel that I was staying at, who drove me to the Ministry of Health in Sandviken. From there I researched the dates and measurements of radioactivity following the accident. She also helped me by telephoning biologists at several universities who would perhaps have known of anybody undertaking research on the effects of Chernobyl on nature. Talking to some on the phone, I heard them claim that the doses were too small to cause morphological disturbances. One biologist in Gävle claimed that research such as mine was not necessary. It was only years later that I learnt of Prof. Anssi Saura's study, at the University of Umeo, who found a high mutation rate of Drosophila in Gävle.[4]

It was estimated in the western literature of the time that 1 rem per hour was measured in the close area around Pripjat. In itself this was a lot, but unofficial sources claimed even higher measurements.[5] Information was very scarce, except for measurements made in Switzerland.

Ticino

for what is called a 'wash out' (normally, 50% of the active particles are washed out by 5 mm of rain in a 24 hour period. In cases of 20 mm this figure rises to 95%). In Ticino, between April 30 and May 4 1986 the amount of rain measured was 58.3 mm. On the night of May 1 radioactivity was detected for the first time. In the villages of Melano, Mendrisio and Chiasso, 21 kBq/m2 (21,000 Bq/m2) of Caesium-137 was measured on May 5 1986.[1]

On September 6 1987 I went to Melano, next to Lago Maggiore. It was still forbidden to swim there, or to eat fish and mushrooms.

Since it was a beautiful autumn it was easy to collect a great number of bugs from different families. Misshapen species were found: limbs and feelers were melted together; the last limb small and soft; one limb missing within the feeler, but at almost normal length, at larval stage; disturbances on feet and legs; wings of uneven lengths; curved bodies. On October 3 I returned to the area, this time staying in Rancate. In Mendrisio, one of the larger towns, I collected many strangely-formed leaves that had heavy disturbances.

In order to increase my experience of the possible misshapes, such as these, that had resulted from the Chernobyl fallout I decided to collect fruit flies (Drosophila) in Rancate, in order to breed them at home in bottles with special food (such as they use in the laboratories of the University in Zürich). I collected three pairs of Drosophila melanogaster. The males and females can be easily distinguished by their appearance. I had drawn and painted them during my career as a scientific illustrator at the Zoological Institute of Zürich for many publications - dead as well as alive - directly from the bottles. The flies were kept in bottles over several Generations, never displaying deformities unless they were specially mutated for an experiment.

Back in Zürich on October 13, the two pairs of Drosophila had laid their eggs in the bottles which I had kept for breeding them in.

On October 14 Mendrisio I and Mendrisio III (as I

Having observed misshapen bugs in areas of Sweden such as Gysinge, I decided to collect bugs in an area which had received approximately one quarter of this amount of fallout from Chernobyl. Consequently I travelled to Ticino, in the southern part of Switzerland next to the Italian border (in fact Italian is spoken in Ticino).

On May 1 1986 the dry fallout from Chernobyl came down. Between May 2 and 4 a heavy rain was responsible called the stocks) showed small larvae, or the food had been disturbed (meaning that the larvae had come out of their eggs but were so tiny that one could not yet see them). No larvae were visible in the Mendrisio II bottle.

On October 16 I put the parents in new bottles labelled 'original parents'. I had not examined the parents as I would have had to anaesthetise them, and I didn't want to take any risks of disturbing their breeding. When they died my inspection showed that they looked undamaged.

On October 21 the first Generation slipped out of the pupa. I made two new bottles for some of the flies, labelling them Mendrisio I and Mendrisio III, 1. Generation. Still nothing happened in Mendrisio II.

From the 1. Generation I looked at 6 flies from Mendrisio I. There were 3 males and 3 females; all looked healthy. On October 30 I looked at 56 flies from the Mendrisio I 1. Generation. Fly 29, a male, had segments in complete disorder, and the bristles on the heads of other flies were uneven in length.

On November 1 I looked at 106 flies from Mendrisio III 1. Generation. The insects Nr. 6 and 7 showed deformations on the abdomen, bristles and thorax. Nr. 12 had a heavily misshapen face, and the trunk (proboscis) was missing. Nr. 18 had the right postverticals turned and shorter. Nr. 20 had wings that were turned upwards in a spoon shape. Nr. 23 had a shrunken wing which in every other respect looked normal. The bristles on the thorax of Nr. 26 were not normal. Nr. 27 had disturbances on segments of the abdomen. Nr. 28 had black dots on the first segment of the abdomen. Nr. 36 lacked some bristles on the thorax. Nr. 37 had deformations on the segments of the abdomen. Nr. 58 had deformations on the face, third feeler limb right side too short, the eye not at all right. Nr. 73 had deformations on segments on the abdomen. Nr. 87 had a deformation on the segments on the abdomen. Nr. 89 had disturbances of the face and eyes; the face had caved in. Nr. 104 had disturbances of the face.

On November 4 I looked at 162 flies from the bottle Mendrisio I 1. Generation. Group 1, 22 flies were well.

Group II Nr. 16 bristles on the head were in uneven length. The bristle on the head of Nr. 24 had snapped. Group III: the wing of Nr. 3 was wavy, with too many bristles. On Nr. 7 the left bristle on the scutellum was too short. Nr. 14 had disturbances of the bristles on the head. On the right side of Nr. 16 the vibrissae (which normally looks like a little brush) was missing. On Nr. 22 the carina (the carina looks like a nose) was pointed at the lower end, and dark. The bristles on the face of Nr. 25 were lacking. Group IV: on Nr. 6 the left side of the scutellum (the shield forming the triangle between the insect's wings), one bristle was too long. The bristle on the thorax of Nr. 8 was missing. Nr. 10 lacked the ocelli (three little points on the flies' head. Ocellus is a general term for several types of 'simple eye' as found in insects. These are usually incapable of image formation). On Nr. 12 a bristle was missing on the left side of the thorax . On Nr. 21 three bristles on the thorax were missing. On Nr. 26 there was an additional bristle on the thorax. Group V: on Nr. 7 one bristle next to the ocelli was missing. On Nr. 25 one bristle on the thorax was too short. On Nr. 28 one bristle on the thorax was missing. Group VI: on Nr. 2 and 7 one bristle on the thorax was missing. On Nr. 12 two bristles on the thorax were missing. On Nr. 21 the left bristle on the scutellum was too short. On Nr. 24 two bristles on the thorax were missing.

Mendrisio II 1. Generation had disturbances on the segments of the abdomen, disturbances of the face and proboscis, particles of eye pigments on the heads, and misshapen eye forms.

Mendrisio I and II, 2. Generation. I found many deformations on the wings, spoon-like shapes, one wing crumpled like a small ball.

Overall, Mendrisio I showed more disturbances of the abdomen, Mendrisio III more of the wings.

I went to Professor Nöthiger, at the University of Zürich, to show him a small bottle of disturbed flies, but he was not interested in looking at them. In January 1988 I published an article with paintings of the bugs, flies and leaves in a Swiss magazine.[2] The reaction of the scientists was hostile.

Canton Aargau

A Canton is a division of Swiss territory (constituted with a separate small-scale government with legislative and executive powers, which is still responsible to the federal government). Three nuclear power plants are located in the Canton of Aargau (which lies in the north and middle of Switzerland): Leibstadt, a boiling water reactor, and Beznau I and II, which are pressurised water reactors. In addition there is a nuclear research institute with one reactor, that had been shut down in December 1993. Outside the border of the Canton of Aargau, in the Canton of Solothurn, there is another boiling water reactor called Gösgen. The main wind direction from it is towards the Canton of Aargau.

Before the Chernobyl accident I never once thought about the dangers of nuclear power plants. In Switzerland there was a strong anti-nuclear opposition, which even prevented the building of two new power plants which had been proposed. There are still people who, on a private basis, measure radioactivity around the Swiss plants.

In the summer of 1988 I took up my search around the Gösgen and Leibstadt power plants, in order to find out how the leaf bugs looked. Steam emanating from the cooling towers (evaporating coolant water) was visible from many parts of the countryside, and I tried to detect the wind directions and which parts of the Canton could be affected. As architectural constructions the power plants impressed me with their hugeness; their spherical, cubed and cylindrical forms.

My first stop on June 27 1988 was near the power plant Gösgen, where I collected 41 insects, and a Drosophila melanogaster. Of these 10 were damaged. The Drosophila had one feeler shorter than the other, and the eyes did not have the same shape. Two leaf bugs had one wing shorter than the other. There were abnormal forms of feelers and legs, and a growth out of an eye. It looked shocking and terrible. From there I walked in the main wind direction to Baden, which is about 30 km away from Gösgen, and stopped at several spots to collect insects.

Around Beznau I found 31 insects, 1 of which had crumpled wings. The rest looked fine. It was very difficult to find any leaf bugs around the power plant, which was surprising as the plants looked healthy and were the right ones. I started to concentrate more on the other power plants.

I walked around the Leibstadt plant several times. In the area surrounding the power plant I found bugs with disturbances on both feelers and wings of uneven lengths, as well as misshapen abdomens and crippled legs and feet. However, across the Rhein River, in Germany, I could not find any damaged insects.

Throughout my search I also collected plant leaves that showed interesting irregularities and asymmetric forms. The veins in the leaves showed knots, and these forms had strange variations. I also found these and other leaves near Chernobyl, which I later used for a series of paintings; comparing the leaf forms from Leibstadt with the ones that I had found in Chernobyl.

I published this work in April 1989, in the same magazine, Tages-Anzeiger, that I had been published in a year before.[1]

Included in the article was a text by entomologist Prof. Sauter ETH declaring that he was worried by my findings. He stated that, normally, in order to find one misshapen bug one had to look at a great number of individual ones, and concluded that a study should be made. An additional text by Ralph Graeub, who had already published a book about the effects of low artificial radiation and the Petkau Effect[2] in 1985, pointed out that the dangers of radioactivity in low doses are underestimated; that visible cancer cases could be just the peak of the iceberg, and that other symptoms and illnesses are often unseen. He concluded that change and aberration in chromosomes should be studied more thoroughly. The third person to write was Prof. Nöthiger, who stated that I was claiming the liberty to express myself on a scientific subject with no knowledge of what I was speaking about; in effect having a 'fool's license', meaning that I could do whatever I wanted without any responsibility, like a king's fool. It was hard for him to respond because in his eyes my work was emotional and operated with preconceived ideas that disparage normal-working power plants. He claimed that disturbances in nature are normal and mutations happen with a frequency of 0.2 to 1 percent.

In my article I didn't give any numbers or percentages of the disturbed bugs. I didn't want to be pseudo-scientific, but it was exactly this lack of numbers that resulted in the worst reproaches being made against me by the scientific community. Prof. Nöthiger claimed that the radioactivity from the Chernobyl fallout - in 1986 a 20 mrem average for the Swiss population per year - was much less than natural radiation (135 mrem); and, in addition, that the radioactivity from normal working power plants was even lower. He therefore appeared to think that the only reason for me to do this work was to frighten people; still a standard reaction of most biologists. There is still no comparable work on this topic.

The reaction to my article in the media was incredible. Overnight I had become an 'official' person. Radio and TV asked for interviews. Even outside of Switzerland there was a great response. At the same time it frightened me to stand there all by myself with this supposedly 'unscientific' article, vulnerable to waves of anger and reproaches at my back. Prof. Sauter had at least looked at the insects I had shown him from Sweden and Ticino, and was impressed. Prof. Nöthiger refused to even look at the first generation of Mendrisio flies, which I had put on his desk. The invitation to me in his article - to help me now with my work - seemed hollow, and I didn't dare step into his laboratory again.

What had I done? Was I just a plain crazy fool?

In the summer of 1989 I again spent a great deal of time around Leibstadt, Ticino and Sellafield; asking myself whether I had perhaps become crazy. I searched for leaf bugs, travelled, walked around and painted as much as I possibly could. In 1990 I had a big show in the Graphic Collection of the Federal Technical Institute ETH in Zürich. A text which Prof. Hohl of the Graphic Collection had written for the exhibition (and which went to the press) was corrected by the head of the scientific department of the ETH, smoothing over everything that sounded provocative.

The parliamentarian Hansjürg Weder from Basel, terrified by my findings and the pictures of the damaged leaf bugs, stated that a study should be made. Eventually, and with three professors from the ETH, I was allowed go on a tour, showing them the places where I had found the insects. They came to the conclusion that no ill insects should be found in these beautiful spots.

The Bundesrat (the highest government in Switzerland) decided that a second study should be made. The zoologist Dr. J. Jenny conducted the study and gave me leaf bugs to paint (which I did of my own accord with no financial renumeration. I did everything out of my personal engagement with the work). At the beginning I was very happy to have someone who was knowledgable of, and competent with, insects. I asked him for leaf bugs to paint. The idea was to integrate my paintings into his dissertation. I was, however, very disappointed with the results. His dissertation attempted to make me an object of ridicule, going as far as claiming that I was unable to differentiate between a bug that had just renewed its skin and one which is very light in colour (such as one I had painted at Checkpoint Charlie in the Ukraine). Whilst he didn't really disagree with my findings - he himself found equally great numbers of disturbed leaf bugs - he said that there was no correlation to be made between the high numbers found around nuclear plants and the radiation emitted from the power plants, and that he had found equal numbers of deformations in other parts of the country. However, as he made no distinction between types of misshapes, or locations where they were found, it was not possible to deduce anything from his work. Whilst his dissertation did not name the places where he had found the disturbed leaf bugs, my own work demonstrated that varied and increasingly worse malformations could be found closer, rather than further away, from the power plants. He also used colour prints of my work in his exhibition without my permission, omitting contextual information from underneath the paintings.

I felt I had to go on on my own, despite the constant - and very offensive - anger of the Swiss biologists that I had encountered.

Sellafield

I chose Sellafield in Great Britain for a study because of the bad reputation the plant had, and also because most of the nuclear waste from Switzerland is reprocessed there.

At the time I was still beginning my work and, unsure, felt the need to investigate matters in line with prevailing scientific views: specifically, that high radiation caused the worst deformities. I was ready to believe that a plant which emitted more radioactivity than a Swiss plant (I was still convinced at the time that the Swiss plants were the best!) would cause worse deformities since the radioactivity expelled into the atmosphere is higher. In fact later comparisons showed that the deformities were equally bad. When I first showed the scientists the results of my work I thought that they would cheer; when their reaction was negative I began to more overtly disagree with them. After the Sellafield study I decided to go my own way.

On October 10 1957 one of the first serious accidents in the history of nuclear power plants occurred at Sellafield (called Windscale at the time). High doses of radioactive waste escaped through the chimneys and polluted a vast area stretching as far as Norway. On October 11 there was still no public warning about the dangerous Polonium-210 that had been emitted. It was only later, in an area covering 200 square miles, that milk was thrown out for 44 continuous days by order of the government, in order to avoid contaminating the population with J-131.

The reports on the many 'small' and 'negligible' mishaps at Sellafield after that period read like a criminal story.

Just to pick out a few examples: on January 28 1986 Sellafield British Nuclear Fuels Limited explained to Greenpeace that only a small amount of uranium (440 kg) - well below the government authorised levels - was discharged into the Irish Sea with the approval of the Nuclear Inspectorate.[1] On February 5 1986 BNFL put its Windscale reprocessing plant at Sellafield, Cumbria, on amber alert, only two weeks after nearly half a tonne of uranium was dumped into the Irish Sea from the plant. The incident happened in the huge decanning plant where spent uranium rods from nuclear power stations are stripped down ready for reprocessing. The alert, the second of four warning stages, was the first since an incident in 1973. Reports from outside the plant suggested that between 50 and 60 people were contaminated after breathing a radioactive cloud or mist from a pump which was undergoing maintenance. Seventy workers at Sellafield were checked for contamination but initial tests using face and nose swabs were negative. The plant's 'whole body' monitor was on standby if needed.[2] The company emphasised that the release was contained within the plant, and that staff responded according to plant procedures, which included the evacuation of 'non-essential' workers - only on Friday February 7, BNFL admitted that plutonium nitrate had escaped into the atmosphere.[3] On February 14 1986, BNFL investigated the cause of a fire that occurred on February 13 at the nuclear waste disposal site in Drigg, near the Sellafield reprocessing plant in Cumbria.[4] In October 1988 scientists at the Sellafield nuclear reprocessing plant admitted that there had been a radioactive leak into the ground from a chemical separation unit.[5] In March 1989 little Gemma D'Arcy of Cleator was dying of leukaemia. Her mother claimed that the illness had been provoked by radioactivity from Sellafield.[6]

In 1983 a Yorkshire television crew discovered that there were many children ill with leukaemia in Seascale, near Sellafield. The statistics of such a high incidence of leukaemia had been lost within the larger district. In 1990 Martin Gardner, of the University of Southampton, made a study in which 52 cases of leukaemia, 22 cases of Non-Hodgkin-Lymphoma and 23 cases of Hodgkin Lymphogranulomatose had occurred between the years 1950 to 1985 in patients under the age of 25 years. Comparison with a separate control group of 1001 people of the same age showed that the number of ill children was above the expected rate.

Gardner suggested that there was a correlation between those fathers working in the Sellafield plant - and radiation induced mutations suffered - and the childrens' illnesses. He also indicated that the risk of plant workers' children becoming ill with leukaemia or Non-Hodgkin-Lymphoma was up to 6 to 8 times above the average.

I installed myself in a bed-and-breakfast in Holmrook near Sellafield on July 8 1989, and started collecting insects on the day I arrived. The next morning I began to paint a seven point ladybird with black patches and crumpled wings. After buying a map of the area and observing the winds, I made plans about where I wanted to collect the bugs.

I started in Seascale next to the stone ring, and found 28 insects, bugs, beetles and flies, 4 of which had deformations on the feelers and wings of uneven lengths. In observing that the wind came from the sea to the land, on an opposite hillside near Ponsonby, on July 30 I collected 34 insects, 5 of which had disturbances. I recorded the worst deformations on one bug larva of the soft family Miridae, which had a heavy deformation on the right wings, a seven point ladybird with wings of uneven length, and a leaf hopper which had a hole between the head and the thorax. In Strands, way up in the mountains near the Wast Water Lake (where the drinking water for the area comes from), I collected 34 insects, all of which were all right except one. In Ravenglass, south of Sellafield, I found only 7 insects, all of which were all right. On July 31 I went up the mountains again, this time to Wast Water Lake, collecting only 15 leaf bugs, one of which had feelers with little knots. The vegetation and landscape were very beautiful.

On August 2 I went to the Visitors Center in Sellafield and got a bus tour of the plant. Looking out of the window of the bus, my eye was offended by boxes, wires and rugs lying around, and I hoped that they kept the plant cleaner inside. The lady who was guiding the tour explained, with pride, that the annual amount of radioactive waste produced was as small as the tennis ball she was holding in her hand, and that much less waste was created than by other forms of energy production.

I also learnt that Switzerland contributed financially to a new building at Sellafield for reprocessing waste from Swiss and other European nuclear power plants (in which the waste could be cast into glass). In order to clean the water coming out of the site, it is driven through volcanic rock. The female guide on the bus admitted proudly that within the rock a chemical process takes place that makes the water almost drinkable and that, in addition, the USA had copied their system.

On August 4 I collected 35 insects in Egremont, a large town north of Sellafield, all of which were well. In Seascale and Drigg, I found 23 insects, 3 of which were disturbed. One soft bug had a growth on the right feeler, and another one had dark spots and a misshapen thorax. On August 6 in Calder Bridge I collected 21 insects, 4 of which were disturbed. A leaf hopper had a depression on the head and the wings were crumpled. On the way back I collected 9 more insects in Ponsonby, of which one was a leaf hopper with a short leg with a normal foot on it.

On August 10, at another spot in Drigg, I collected 33 insects, 11 of which were disturbed. I found deformations both on feelers and wings. I observed men working with machines on something that initially looked like a street. When I asked them what it was they told me that a pipeline from the Drigg waste disposal site to the sea was being built. I almost fainted thinking about what might drift into the sea once it was finished.

Near the site on the Seascale side on August 14 I found 27 insects, 7 of which were misshapen. I found some growths on the genitals and the thorax of the bugs, as well as wavy - rather than flat - wings and a larva with dark spots.

In spite of the heavy winds, one could detect that the places with the highest incidence of deformities were in the areas close around Sellafield, or in the main wind directions: such as Seascale, Drigg, Calder Bridge and Ponsonby.

Chernobyl

The experiment at the Chernobyl power plant which began on April 25, 1986, led to the worst imaginable catastrophe, which started on April 26 at 1:24 a.m local time.

On August 12 1990 I went to the contaminated area around Chernobyl with a group of Swiss parliamentarians and journalists. A doctor of our group had an instrument to measure the radioactivity. Arriving at the hotel in Kiev I went outside, where there were many places growing with wild plants, to collect some bugs. I had a microscope with me that I intended to give to Dr. Shcherback of 'GreenWorld' (a group dedicated to fighting against pollution, and specifically against the use of radioactive fuel). I also had everything I needed to collect and paint the bugs. The few bugs and two flies that I looked at late in the evening were morphologically healthy. They were only dirty, and their wings were not shiny, as is usual. That day in Kiev a radiation measurement of 0.04 mSv/h (Millisievert per hpur) was recorded. Next day we rode in buses to the Chernobyl Plant, which is 120 km north of Kiev. At the entrance to the 30 km exclusion zone, called 'Checkpoint Charlie', we had to change buses in order not to contaminate the ones from Kiev. The journalists retired for a press conference, and I went off to collect bugs. A measurement of 0.07 mSv/h was recorded by Dr. (of medicine) Martin Walter on his equipment. Nearby there were some wild plants growing, where I found bugs; mostly the fire bug (Pyrrhocoris apterus).

I collected as many living specimens of fire bugs as I could and brought alive them back for the zoologist Johannes Jenny, for comparative study in Switzerland (please refer to earlier chapters).

Later we drove to the Chernobyl Plant, and were invited into the building to listen to several speeches given by the director and scientific staff of the plant. A huge portrait of Lenin was still hanging on the back of the stage. We entered via the main gate, where all the workers go in and out, and are measured before and after work. We measured 91.0 mSv/h at this entrance. There were soldiers with rifles standing around, and it was not possible to collect any bugs. Afterwards we went back to the buses to drive to Pripjat, an empty town where 30.0 mSv/h was measured. Music could be heard from loudspeakers, a measure to keep the guards from going crazy in this ghost city. Looking into the windows of the houses, one could still see breakfast on the table, toys and other utensils; in short, just how everything was left when the citizens were evacuated. The vegetation had started to take over and looked green and healthy. I picked some branches and leaves, which I pressed immediately, and collected only a few bugs, as there were not many to be found. Back at the hotel I examined, using a microscope, a green soft bug with one short and wavy leg. Other soft bugs had wavy wings or thick feelers; one larva had wings of uneven length. It was only when I painted the Robbinia branches that I had collected in Pripjat, once back in Zürich, that I realised how different the little leaves were in length and form. On August 15 we drove to Polesskoje, which is on the west side of the 30 km exclusion zone. There, as in Kiev, the streets were still washed with water several times a day. Since we had some doctors in our group, people gathered around us. Mothers were crying, and asking us to look at their children. One could see that these people were in great distress. Living outside the 30 km exclusion zone, they had not been evacuated, even though the radioactivity was higher (0.60 - 1.01 mSv/h that day) than in some places within the zone. These people had no future, no joy to look forward to; just plain fear. They ate contaminated food every day. Since they did not have equipment to measure the radioactivity the population was unable to identify the most contaminated areas in the town. They were unable to protect their children, who did not know where to even play without fear of contamination.

On August 15 we went to Slavoutich, a new city that had been built for the Chernobyl refugees by all the republics of the Soviet Union (which had still been joined at the time). The workers with the most dangerous work at the Chernobyl plant got one or two family houses; the others were living in ugly apartment blocks. Even though the houses were new they already seemed to be falling apart. There was no doctor for the whole city, only medical aids. They built the town 90 km north of Chernobyl, thinking the soil and water would be clean. However, the medical helpers were completely exhausted by the amount of work and the lack of medication, and were faced with many, many sick children. The town had been built in the clearing of a huge forest. Unfortunately no bugs lived in the forest, and I found only one! One limb was too light a colour, and was too short.

In Kiev, Polesskoje and Slavoutich, I collected leaves and painted them once I was back in Zürich. In the paintings - which were exact copies of the original leaves - the deformations became more visible.

In April 1996 I was invited to Vienna to show my work at the Permanent Peoples' Tribunal, a nomadic forum (comprised of six judges) which groups can go to if they think that their problems are not being heard.[1] The people testifying at the Tribunal were medical doctors, immunologists and radiobiologists from Belarus, the Ukraine and Russia. As a result of the tribunal's findings a book about Chernobyl was produced.[2] Governments and official scientists maintain that illnesses which are hard to describe - head aches, lack of concentration, depression, feelings of pain in the eyes due to normal sunlight, stomach problems, libido problems, tiredness, etc - suffered by people in contaminated areas are only created by the fear of radioactivity from the Chernobyl plant, and the resultant stress; summarising them under the title 'radiophobia'. They also maintain that these illnesses are not, therefore, radiation-related. However, as we heard at the Tribunal, 80% of the exposed population - even in areas with low radiation - suffer from complications of the digestive system, psycho-organic syndromes, high blood-pressure, absent-mindedness, immunological problems, as well as new forms of cancer. In Gomel Belarus, only 2 out of 1500 children were found to be healthy. The accumulated dose is 30-50 Bq/kg per kg weight.[3] Studies by scientists from Russia, Belarus and the Ukraine showed that these illnesses are caused by even the lowest measured radiation in the areas hit by the Chernobyl cloud. Their studies, in effect, support my views.

Prof. E. B. Burlakova states that "radiobiologists have gained a wealth of knowledge on the influence of high doses of ionizing radiation on biomacromolecules, cells and organisms. However, we have no profound understanding or any generally accepted theories of the impact of a slight man-made increase in the ambient radiation levels on the surrounding living nature. It is habitual to use models only and predict the effects of low doses by extrapolation from data on high doses. This seems justified and makes us feel confident, and maybe appropriate for most radiation protection purposes. But even the first experiments on the influence of low dose irradiation on biological systems have shown significant and diversified responses of biosystems in those ranges where we did not expect any effects. Biochemical and biophysical properties of cells, the genome, membranes and the regulatory systems may be altered. Low doses of up to 5 centiSieverts are 20-30 times more efficient than high doses of 100 cSv. The same biological effects of the radiation action is achieved by different ways for low and high radiation doses. As distant consequences one should take account not only of carcinogenic and genetic effects, but also changes in sensitivity to the action of damaging factors of exogenous and endogenous nature resulting in some additional diseases."[4]

Three Mile Island

Three Mile Island lies on the Susquehanna River, about 16 miles from the town of Harrisburg (160,000 population) in the United States. On the morning of March 28, 1979, an accident resulted in large amounts of Iodine-131 and other fission gases being released. At the time of the accident the reactor had only been in use for three months. By a combination of various factors - including a dysfunctional pump, two security system lapses, and a label masking a warning light on a console - the plant's emergency pumps were shut down. Within a few minutes water changed into vapour, and parts of the atomic nucleus were exposed. Temperatures rose and, undetected by workers, Block 2 began to melt down. It was only two days later that Governor Richard Thornburgh ordered an evacuation, a period in which children and pregnant women had been walking outside (the greatest infant mortality rate took place in those areas closest to the plant).

I travelled to Three Mile Island in 1991 to look at the condition of leaf bugs there, propelled by the question of whether there were any visible deformations left from the accident.

I initially looked for windroses of the area (a windrose is a rosette-like diagram showing the relative frequency and strength of the winds in percentage in a locality for given periods of the year). According to the Final Programmatic Environmental Impact Statement of the U.S. Nuclear Regulatory Commission of March 1981, I found that only one wind rose was recorded, dating from 1972-1975, showing that the main wind direction was NNW, NW and WNW. Why was there no windrose from the days after the accident, or information on a map about the recorded radioactivity within the Final Report, I asked myself? A friend of mine gave me a drawing which showed that the highest estimated contour dose in the vicinity of Three Mile Island in a NW direction from March 28 to April 3 was 697 milliRöntgen. Unfortunately this drawing lacked other information: such as distances in miles.

During the cleanup of the Three Mile Island power plant (which is still going on today) the doses of radiation received were calculated for total body and organs, for adults, teenagers, children and infants. The Impact Statement of the US Nuclear Regulatory Commission did not identify the distribution of these doses on any maps, instead referring to the 'nearest garden', the 'nearest goat', etc. At least they listed wind directions to the nearest garden ENE, the nearest cow N, the nearest garden and cow E, etc. It showed that the wind directions were not stable; apart from this, it was not possible to draw any conclusions from the poor quality information that had been made available.

On the day of the accident, March 28, the full dose of the leak hit the population. Mary Osborn, who wrote a report of her own and also made drawings of deformed leaves from the plants in Swatara and other towns, described how she and her husband, working outside early in the morning of the accident, had a 'clean metallic taste' in their mouths and, later that day, sunburn effects on their hands and faces.

During the decontamination and clean up Krypton-85 was released during the period June 28 to July 11, 1980.[1] The point of maximum exposure during the emission was a location about 0.4 miles from the site in an ESE direction (the site is not named). If a person had remained at this location throughout the emission, he/she would have received a beta skin dose of 4.5 mrem and a whole-body gamma dose of 0.05 mrem.[2] The Impact Statement states that the release stopped at 0.4 miles, at the River Road next to the plant; implying that nobody was harmed.

Starting my studies on July 19 and 21 1991, I walked to the closest point to the plant, near Goldsboro (on the opposite bank of the Susquehanna River), in a NW wind direction. I first found 24, and then another 49, insects. Of the initial 24, 5 were damaged on their antenna and legs. Of the 49, 2 were disturbed.

In the N direction of Goldsboro, 32 insects were collected, 3 of which were damaged: one was a leaf hopper which had a growth out of the right eye and red pigment all over the head.

In Swatara, NNW direction on July 23, I picked up 16 insects, 8 of which were damaged. The worst was a leaf bug missing a section of left antenna, but which was the same length as the one on the right side. The vegetation looked sick and dirty, and I thought that the reason was perhaps the pollution from the Bethlehem Steel Corporation which was not far away.

From there I went further up the hill near Oberlin, from where one could see the steam from Three Mile Island. On a nice spot I found 35 insects with ease, 3 of which showed deformations. The worst was a stinkbug which had a misshaped antenna. On July 25 I came back to this place and gathered 31 insects, 4 of which had brown dots on their wings but no deformations.

New Cumberland is a small town, situated south of Harrisburg and in a WNW direction from the Three Mile Island power plant. On my arrival there, and during a search for a bed-and-breakfast, I collected 18 insects, 2 of which looked bad, near a railway bridge. On July 22, on 15th Street, I found 43 insects, all looking well. Later I collected 54 insects all the way up to the Route 83 Highway in New Cumberland, only one of which had a deformation (in this case on one leg).

My first closer approach I made to Three Mile Island was on July 24, on top of the hillside in Londonderry on Geyer/Church Street, in sight of the four cooling towers and their escaping steam (one tower, of course, has had no steam coming from it since the accident). Even though it was a beautiful hidden biotope and it had rained the night before, it was only after a long time that I was able to find a mere 11 insects; 2 of them had black dots on the wings with little holes and disturbances of the chitin. Driving down to Royalton at the shore of the river, I collected 25 insects. Apart from 2 with black dots, they all looked fine. On July 25 I went to the Visitors Center at Three Mile Island, where they tried to convince people how effective nuclear energy is compared to other sources, such as coal, gas or oil.

Half a mile away from Three Mile Island I found a place called Governor's Stable. There I collected 10 insects, 4 of which looked terrible. The worst was a leafbug with only three sections on the left antenna - yet was almost the same length as the one on the right side, as well as a Harlequin bug

with a misshapen scutellum. One ladybird had a large growth on the left wing with a depression. On July 31 I came back to collect 37 insects, 8 of which were deformed, or had dark patches on their bodies. In the neighbourhood of this place, on August 6, I collected another 30 insects, 8 of which were disturbed. On August 2 I drove to Hill/Hess Road, about two and a half miles in an E direction from Three Mile Island. Out of 28 insects, 8 were heavily disturbed. Two ambush bugs had terribly crippled feet, some leaf hoppers had dark brown patches and growths on the wings.

With the freshly caught insects, I usually went back to the bed-and-breakfast in New Cumberland, where I stayed with my microscope and all the painting utensils. After narcotising the insects (a process carried out by dabbing nail polish remover on cotton and exposing the insects to the fumes using a jar system) and making a protocol (a draft of a record about all the insects found on a certain day), I would usually start to paint the insects immediately, as they would otherwise dry out quickly. It was very difficult to gather insects in the neighbourhood of the plant, because "no trespassing" signs were posted everywhere. For a Swiss person this is very unusual, because we can walk wherever we want in the open countryside. Some of the biotopes there were like wild flower gardens with a great variety of butterflies and flowers, a really beautiful sight. But the fear of being caught made me shiver sometimes.

In this project my work involved trying to look for the bugs in the different wind directions, in order to find out where the greatest incidence of disturbed insects were. On a map that I bought I made notes on the spots where I had collected the insects. Looking at these spots I can see they form a rough circle, measuring between 1.5 to 2.5 miles away from the plant (and at other points as far as 8 miles away). By looking at the frequencies of deformations recorded at these different spots I can tell that the worst deformations were only located in the E and ESE direction of the plant and in an area within one mile of the Three Mile Island power plant. No other studies are available.

Krümmel

It is common knowledge today that higher rates of leukaemia and other forms of cancer occur in areas of close proximity to nuclear power plants. Not only near power plants such as Sellafield, but also around the German plants Krümmel, Stade, Würgassen, Neckar 1 and Biblis (here the risk of getting cancer is about 85 times higher than in the rest of Germany). Near the (now closed) Greifswald plant in former East Germany, where 360 billion Becquerels (radiation from the ground) have been measured, the risk of getting cancer was 50 times - and at Rheinsberg 200 times - higher than in areas without nuclear power plants (the statistics of the frequency of risk are compiled by comparison between areas with a nuclear power plant and areas with no nuclear power plant). The plants emit up to 1,000 billion Becquerels of radioactive noble gases and a cocktail of artificial radioactive nuclides.[1] Despite the evidence we have of dead children, the production of radioactive matter is not questioned, but is legal and regarded as normal. Of course, radioactivity in the eyes of the nuclear industry is never responsible for the illnesses around their plants. I ask myself, how many children and adults will have to suffer and die, until our industrial and political systems are ready to look for a new form of renewable energy which doesn't poison all of nature?

Even those scientists who acknowledge that there is the possibility of a link between radioactive pollution and leukaemia tend to explain things in a lengthy and complex manner; their language is hard to read and is also often contradictory, or put in such a way that one can read what one wants to believe in it. Of course, nothing has been proven anyway up to now. A further complicating factor is that epidemiologists from different countries work with different statistical methods, making comparison difficult. British scientists - with the exception of Gardner - have always arrived at negative results which deny the existence of connections between radioactive pollution and cancer, or even that there are leukaemia clusters (a series of cases occurring close together) at all.

The boiling water reactor Krümmel started work in 1984. It is a huge square building with a chimney 148 metres high.

Biological dosimetry - the measurement of radiation in bodies and cells - was performed to find the cause of a cluster of leukaemia victims in the villages of the Elbmarsch, opposite Krümmel at the Elbshore. Between November 1989 and May 1991 five children and one young adult were diagnosed with leukaemia and one child with aplastic anemia. Scientists and epidemiologists compared the affected numbers with expectations of incidence of leukaemia and other forms of cancer for certain age groups: the expectation for children with leukaemia in this period of time would be relatively low. At first scientists thought that there had been an accident in 1988/89; however, the management of Krümmel maintained in public statements that there had been no heavy releases of radioactivity at all.[2]

The Doctor of Environmental Medicine in the Ministry of Health, Dr. M. Csicsaky, said in 1995 that there was room for suspicion as to the cause of the higher rate of leukaemia among these children. He claimed that noble gases, emitted perhaps in higher doses than was permitted (and not by accident, as it was formerly believed), could be responsible for the many ill children in this area.[3]

In Germany, where cancer registration (in which doctors inform a central office of the number of cases recorded throughout the country) has existed since 1980, an epidemiological study was made between 1980 and 1990.[4] It discovered that in the 15 km area around a nuclear power plant there is a statistically relatively higher risk for children contracting leukaemia below the age of 5 years of 1.28. In a 5 km area the relative risk for leukaemia rises to 3.01 for children below the age of 5 years. The study adopted the perspective that the number of children with leukaemia in these areas was small. In spite of these alarming results, the same paper explains why these higher rates of leukaemia have nothing to do with radioactive pollution; based on today's radiobiological knowledge, the amount of radioactive emissions from normal working nuclear power plants is only a fraction of natural radiation, and is therefore not appropriate to provoke any epidemiologically visible accumulation of illnesses.[4] This, in my opinion, reflects the conservative thinking of leading scientists who claim that low radiation from power plants in general - which emit radiation below the doses of natural background radiation - is harmless.

The Krümmel Plant is not marked on the map, but one can find it east of Hamburg at the Elbe River, near the town of Geesthacht.

I stayed in the hotel 'Krümmler Eck', which has a railroad track used for the transport of nuclear waste only 2 metres behind the building. The Elbe is a beautiful river. A strong wind blows of it all day. When I was there the wind became a welcome little breeze in the evening, blowing north to south. With the heavy winds blowing east-west or west-east, one would have thought that all the radioactivity from the Krümmel plant was dispersed into the sky. But the most misshapen insects I found were opposite the Krümmel plant, on the other side of the Elbe, in a western direction.

In the village of Tespe, just opposite the plant on the opposite shores of the Elbe, on July 13 and 17 1995 I collected 66 leaf bugs - 7 of which were damaged - and 31 leaf bugs, 11 of which were damaged. I observed misshapes on feelers and wavy wings. In Obermarschacht, west of Tespe, on July 13 I collected 119 leaf bugs, 13 of which were damaged. Between Tespe and Obermarschacht on July 19, 27 leaf bugs, 11 of which were damaged. The damage was worst in Obermarschacht: a soft bug had, in the larval stage, divided wings; another had a blister on one wing; there were also black patches, and disfigured wings and neckplates. On July 18, east of Krümmel in Tesperhude, I found 56 leafbugs, 3 of which were damaged. The deformities were bent feelers or black patches on wings. North of Tesperhude I collected 50 leaf bugs, 2 of which were damaged, and along the Elbe shore another 28, one of which was damaged. Even further north in Grünhof, 3 km north east of the plant, I collected 20 bugs on July 25, all of which looked well. A pattern became evident: in those areas north of the plant I could only find a few damaged leaf bugs, in contrast to the numbers found to the western side in the Elbmarsch villages.

Behind the forest at Rosenthal road, 2.5 km north-east of the plant, I found 34 leaf bugs, 2 of which were damaged. At the Ziegeleiweg, 2 km north-east of the plant, I found 55 leafbugs, 2 of which were damaged. One squash bug larva was missing a section in one feeler, but both the feelers had the same length. On July 25 at a prehistoric burial site, 3 km east of the plant, I found 18 bugs, all of which were healthy.

On July 24 in Rönne, 4 km west of the plant, 32 bugs were found, all of which looked well. In Krümse, about 6 km west of the plant, I collected 20 leafbugs, 1 of which was disturbed on the legs and had a blister on the ventral side of the thorax.

On July 25 in Geesthacht, along the shore of the Elbe, 56 leaf bugs were found, 3 of which were damaged. A squash bug had a big black growth on the right wing.

It was interesting to see that the damaged bugs were only found in larger numbers in a small stretch of the countryside. The biotopes were quite nice, the weather was hot and dry. The area where the most damaged bugs were found overlaps exactly with the Elbmarsch villages which contained the most ill children and adults. I was shocked when I realised this at the end of the study.

Footnotes

Preface

1   Cornelia Hesse-Honegger, "Ein Opfer von Tschernobyl?", *Tages-Anzeiger Magazin*, Nr.4, 30, January 1988
2   Rosalie Bertell, *No Immediate Danger*, 1985, The Women's Press Ltd
3   Cornelia Hesse-Honegger, "Der Verdacht", *Das Magazin Tages-Anzeiger*, Zürich. Nr. 15, 14/15, April 1989
4   Dr. Johannes Jenny, Eidg. Technische Hochschule ETH, Nr. 10342, "Untersuchungen zu Missbildungerscheinungen an Wanzen (Heteroptera): Erscheinungsformen, Häufigkeit und Bezug zu Schweizer Kernfraftanlagen"
5   Jay. M. Gould, Benjamin A. Godman, "Deadly Deceit", (Ed.) *Four Walls, Eight Windows*, New York 1991
6   UNSCEAR 1982
7   Dr. Ivan Bubriak, "Abstract Forschungsbericht" Paul Scherrer Institut ETH Villigen 1991

Sweden

1   Galina A. Drozdova, M.D. Russian People Friendship University Moscow
2   Galina A. Drozdova, M.D. Russian People Friendship University Moscow
3   Zhores Medwedjew, *Das Vermächtnis von Tschernobyl*, Basil Blackwell, Oxford 1990 and Daedalus Münster 1991
4   Prof. Anssi Saura and Bo Johansson, "Genetic load in northern populations of Drosophila subobscura", *Hereditas* 112, 283 - 287, 1990
5   Zhores Medwedjew, *Das Vermächtnis von Tschernobyl*, Basil Blackwell, Oxford 1990 and Daedalus Münster 1991

Ticino

1   "Radioaktivitätsmessungen in der Schweiz nach Tschernobyl und ihre wissenschaftliche", *Interpretation Tagungsbericht Band 1*, Universität Bern 20 - 22 October, 1986
2   Cornelia Hesse-Honegger, "Ein Opfer von Tschernobyl?", *Tages-Anzeiger Magazin*, Nr. 4, 30, January 1988

Canton Aargau

1   Cornelia Hesse-Honegger, "Der Verdacht", *Das Magazin Tages-Anzeiger, Zürich*, Nr. 15, 14/15, April 1989
2   Ralph Graeub, "Der Petkau Effekt", *Katastrophale Folgen der niedrigen Radioaktivität*, Zytglogge Bern 1985 / 1990

Sellafield

1   *The Guardian*, January 28 1996
2   *The Guardian*, February 6 1996
3   *The Guardian*, February 7 1996
4   *The Guardian*, February 14 1996
5   *The Journal*, October 8 1989
6   *The Journal*, March 18 1989

Chernobyl

1   The Permanent Peoples Tribunal office is located at Via Dogana Vecchia 5, Rome 1-00100 Italy.
2   ISBN 00-001534-5
3   Galina A. Drozdova, M.D. Russian People Friendship University Moscow
4   Prof. e. Burlakova, Institute of Chemical Physics, Moscow, *Radiation Protection Dosymetrie*, vol. 62, 1995

Three Mile Island

1   The Final Programmatic Environmental Impact Statement of the U.S. Nuclear Regulatory Commission, Normal Operations 5.2.4.1., March 1981
2   The Final Programmatic Environmental Impact Statement of the U.S. Nuclear Regulatory Commission, Normal Operations 5.2.3.2., March 1981

Krümmel

1   Echt Knackig, *Der Spiegel* 37, 1994
2   Prof. I. Schmitz-Feuerhake, H. Boetticher, Bremer 1 Institut für Präventionsforschung und Sozialmedizin Leukämieerhöhung im Nahbereich des Siedewasserreaktors Krümmel (Hrsg.) W. Koelzer, R. Maushart Band II, 26. Jahrestagung, Fachverband für Strahlenschutz, Karlruhe, May 1994
3   *Cuxhavener Nachrichten* 30, September 1995
4   Jörg Michaelis, Günter Haaf, Peter Kaatsch und Brigit Keller, Krebserkrankungen im Kindesalter in der Umgebung westdeutscher kerntechnischer Anlagen Deutsches Ärzteblatt, Heft 30, 2538 - 2544, July 24 1992

Paintings

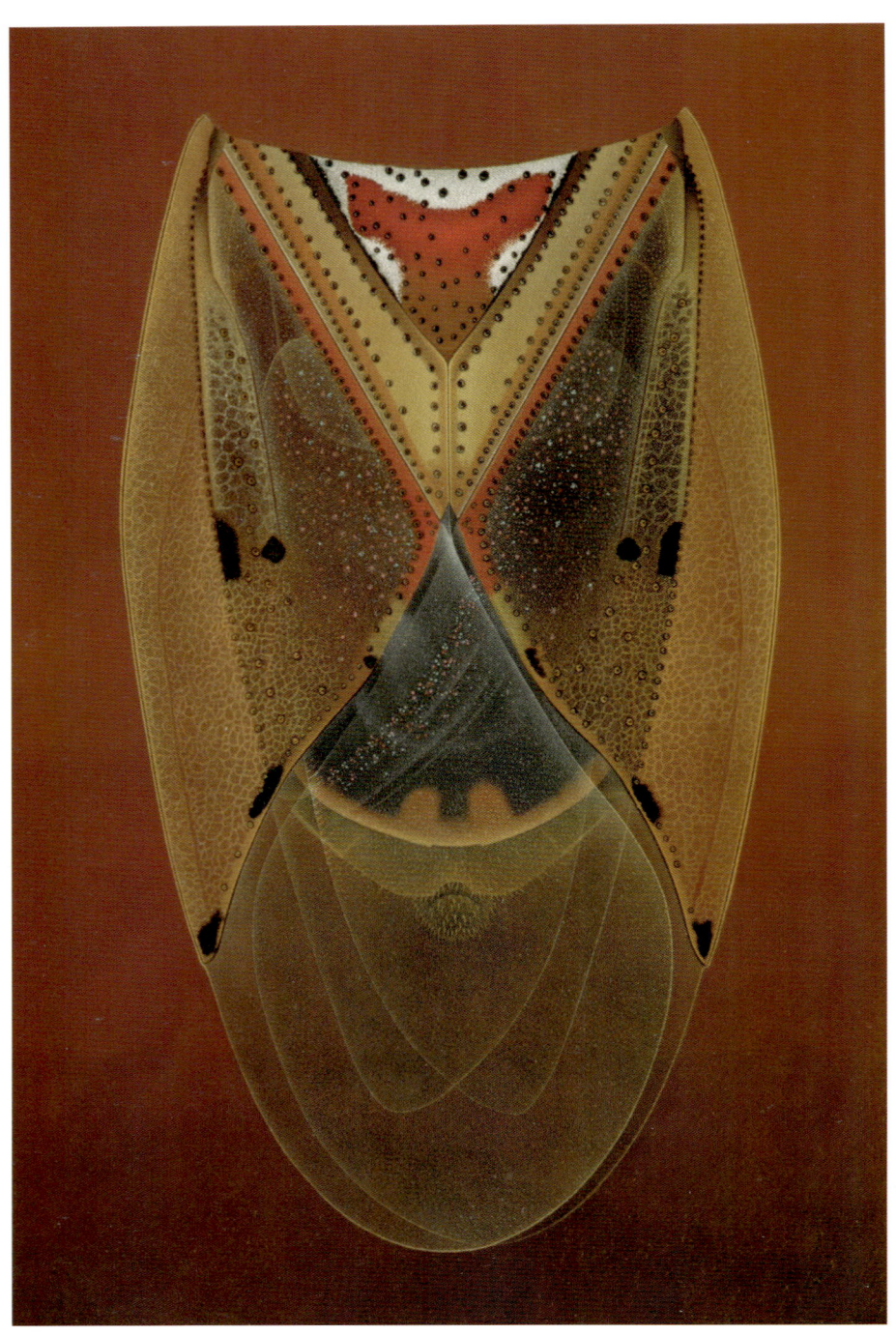

Leaf bug (Miridae, Kleidocerys resedae).
Normal.
Found and painted in Gockhausen.
1978-79. 42cm x 29.7cm.

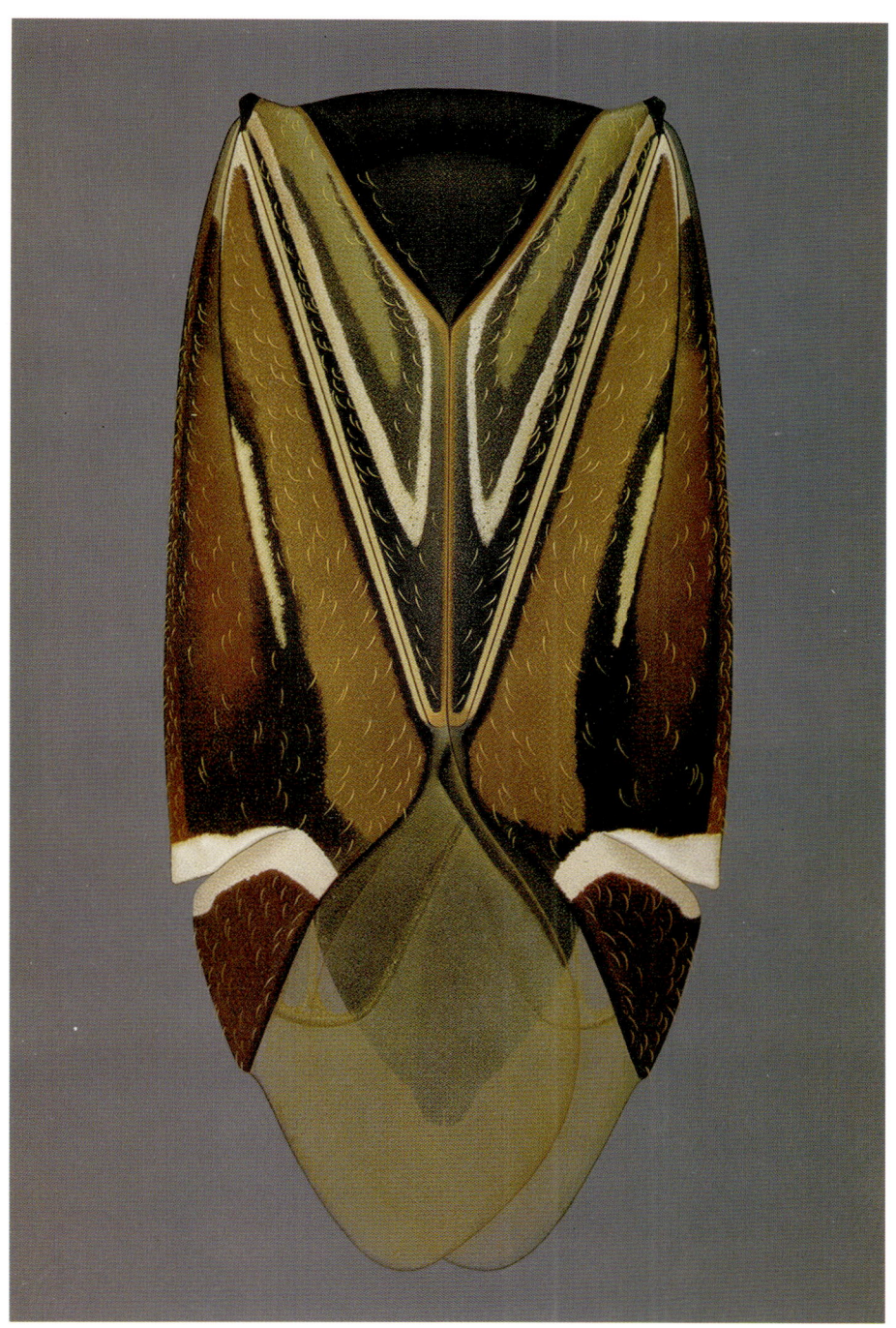

Leaf bug (Miridae, Cremnocephalus).
Normal.
Found and painted in Gockhausen.
1978-79. 42cm x 29.7cm.

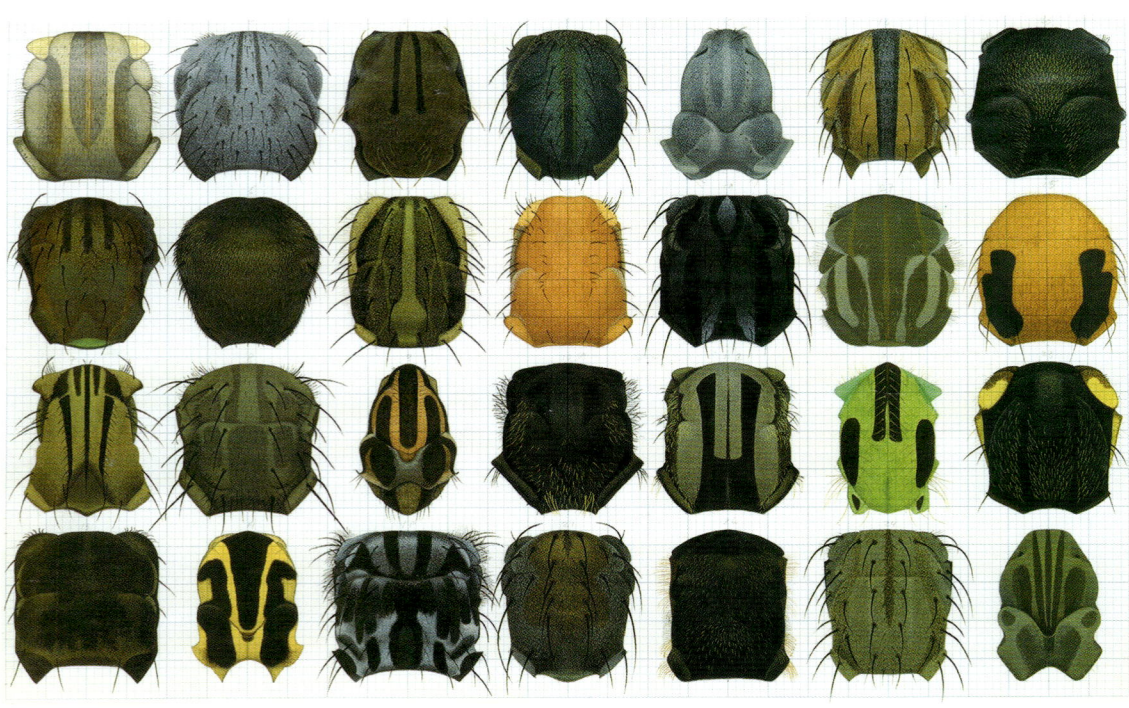

Healthy flies (Diptera, several species).
Painted in non-random pattern. The scutellum have been omitted.
Found and painted in Gockhausen.
1978. 21cm x 29.7cm

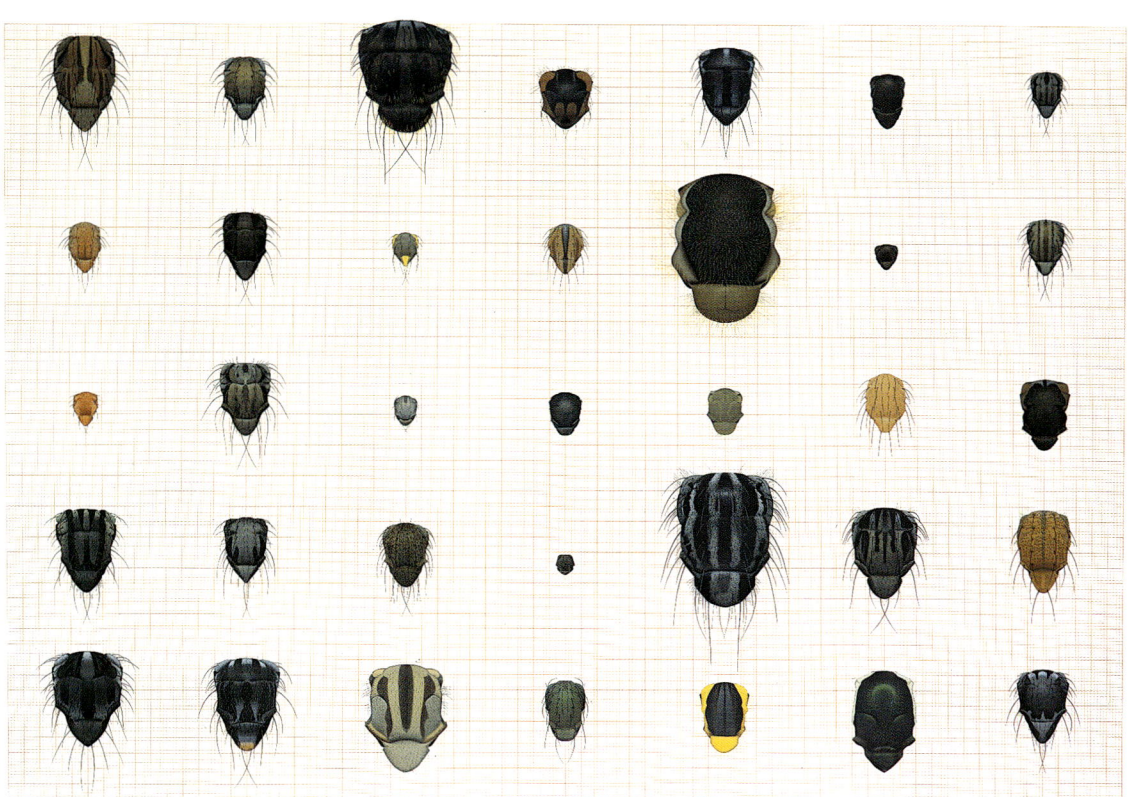

Healthy flies (Diptera, several species).
Backs of flies painted in proportion to each other. The first picture that I made in this way.
Found and painted in Gockhausen.
1981-82. 54.2cm x 74cm

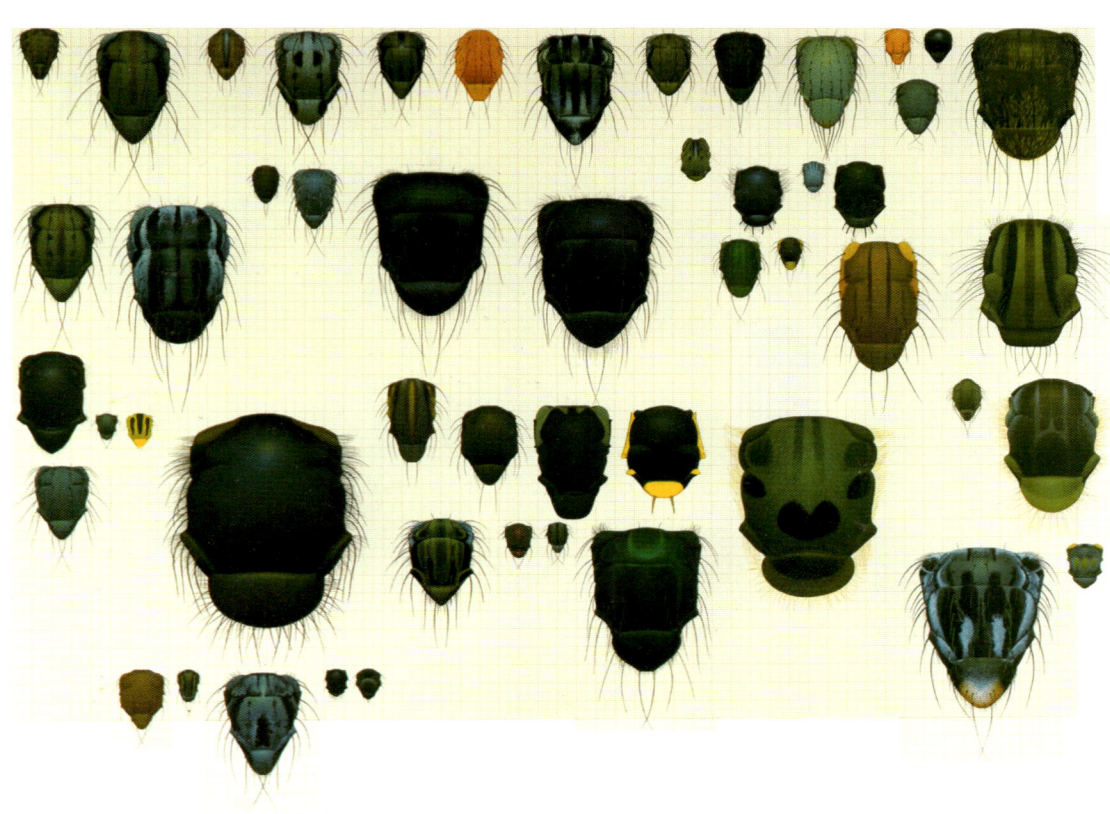

Healthy flies (Diptera, several species).
Backs of flies painted in a random system.
Found and painted in Gockhausen.
1983-85. 45.3cm x 57cm

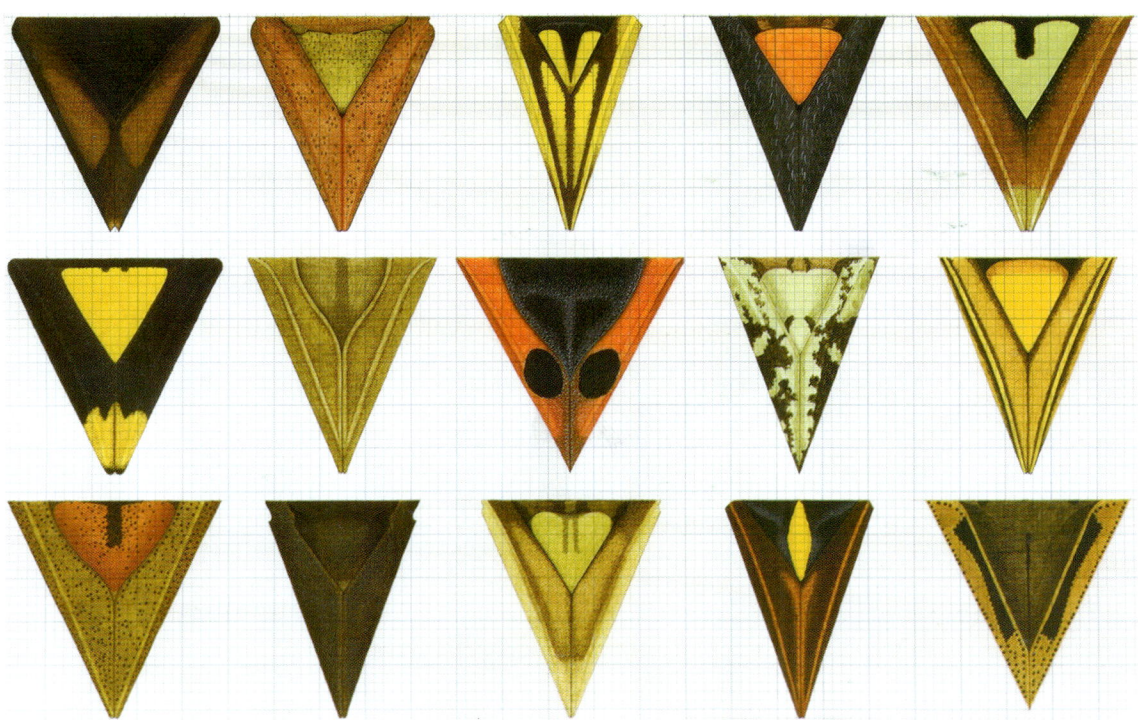

Leaf bug, shields (Miridae, several species).
The upper line towards the neck plate is painted in a straight line.
Found and painted in Gockhausen.
1979. 21cm x 29.7cm.

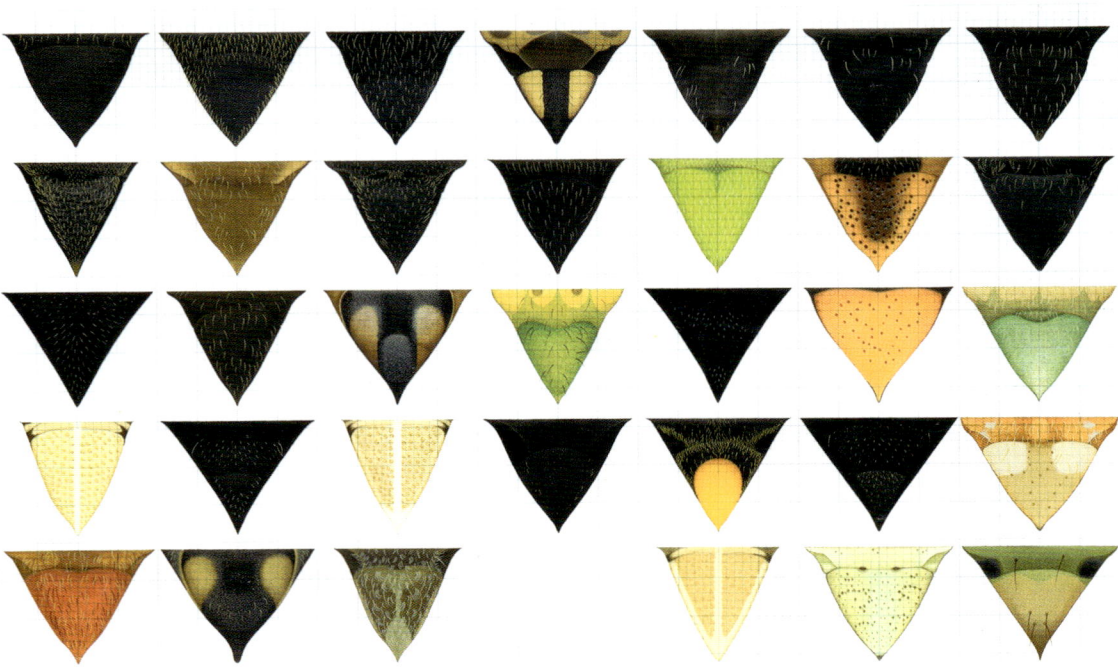

Leaf bugs (Miridae, several species).
Part of the wing and scutellum.
Found and painted in Gockhausen.
1979. 21cm x 29.7cm.

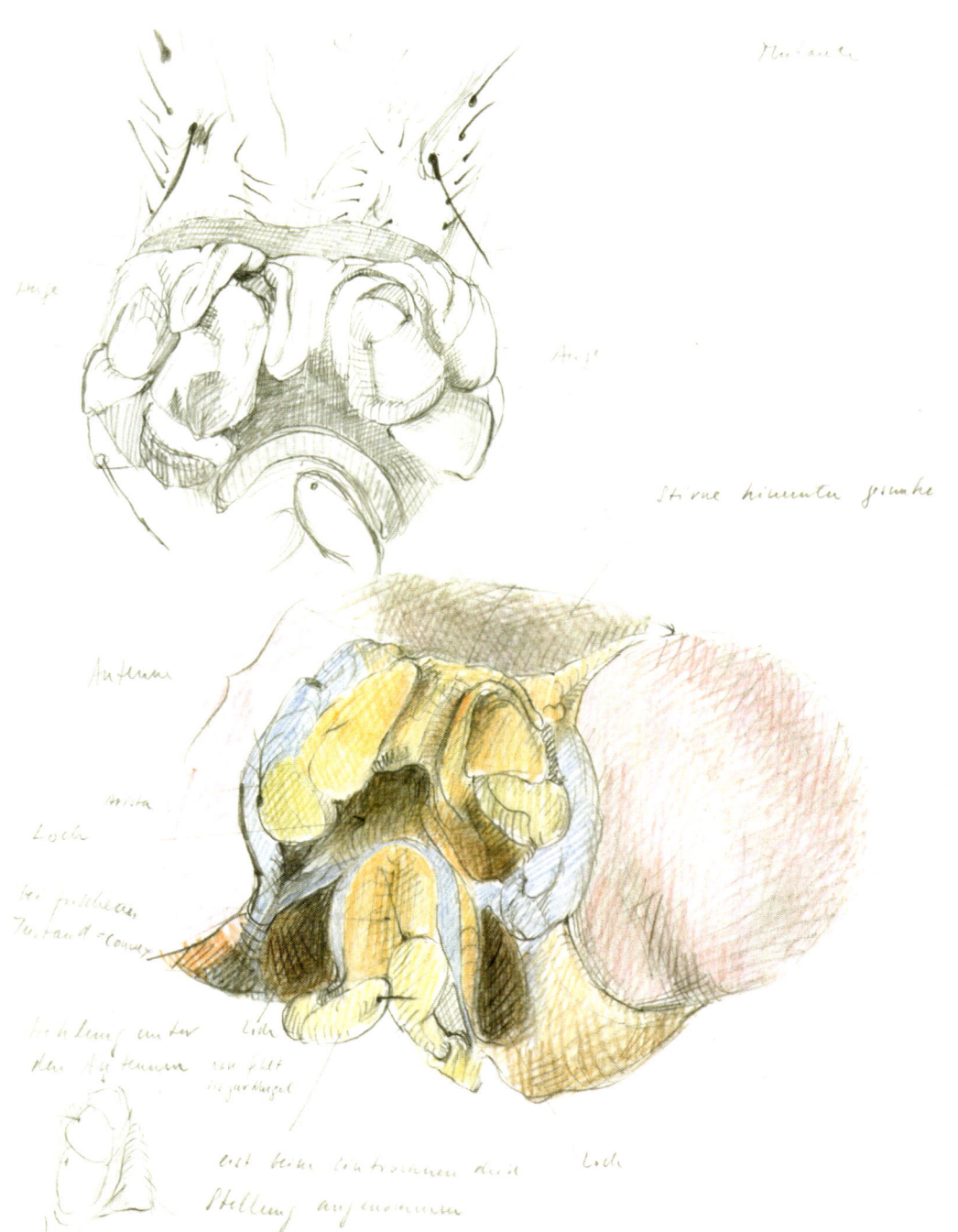

Laboratory flies, heads (Drosophila subobscura mutation - 'quasimodo').
Sketch.
University of Zürich.
1967. 29.7cm x 21cm.

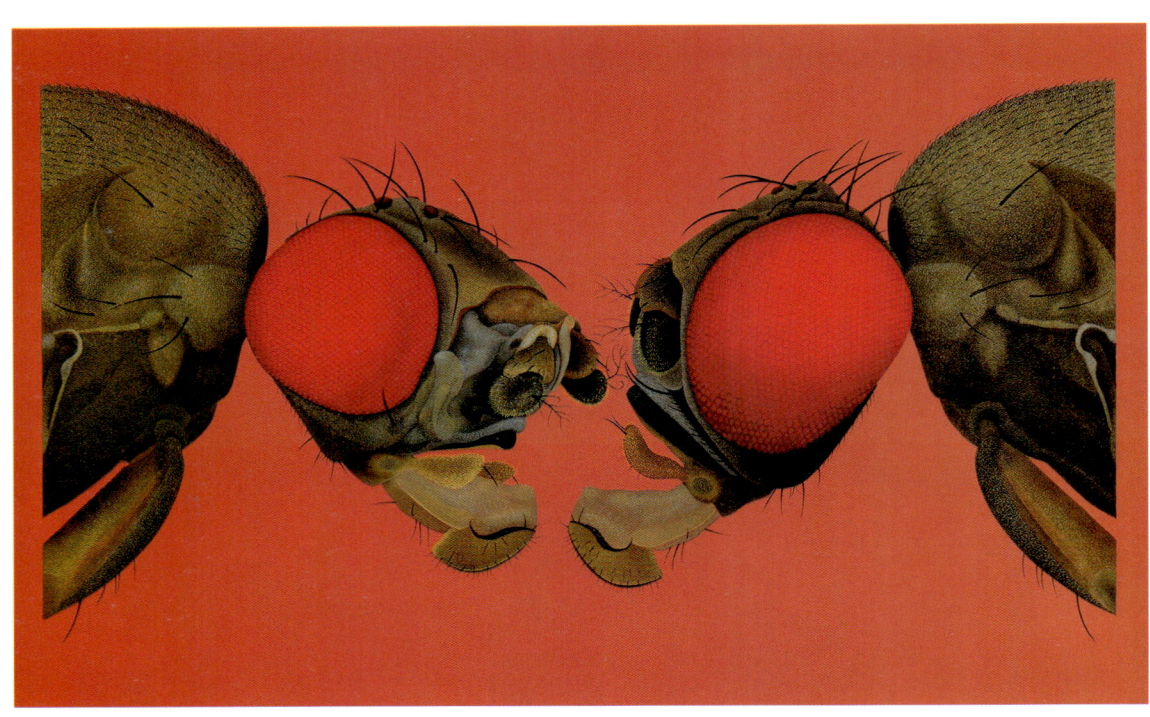

Laboratory flies, heads.
Left: Drosophila subobscura mutation - 'quasimodo'. Right: healthy fly.
University of Zürich.
1967. 42cm x 60cm.

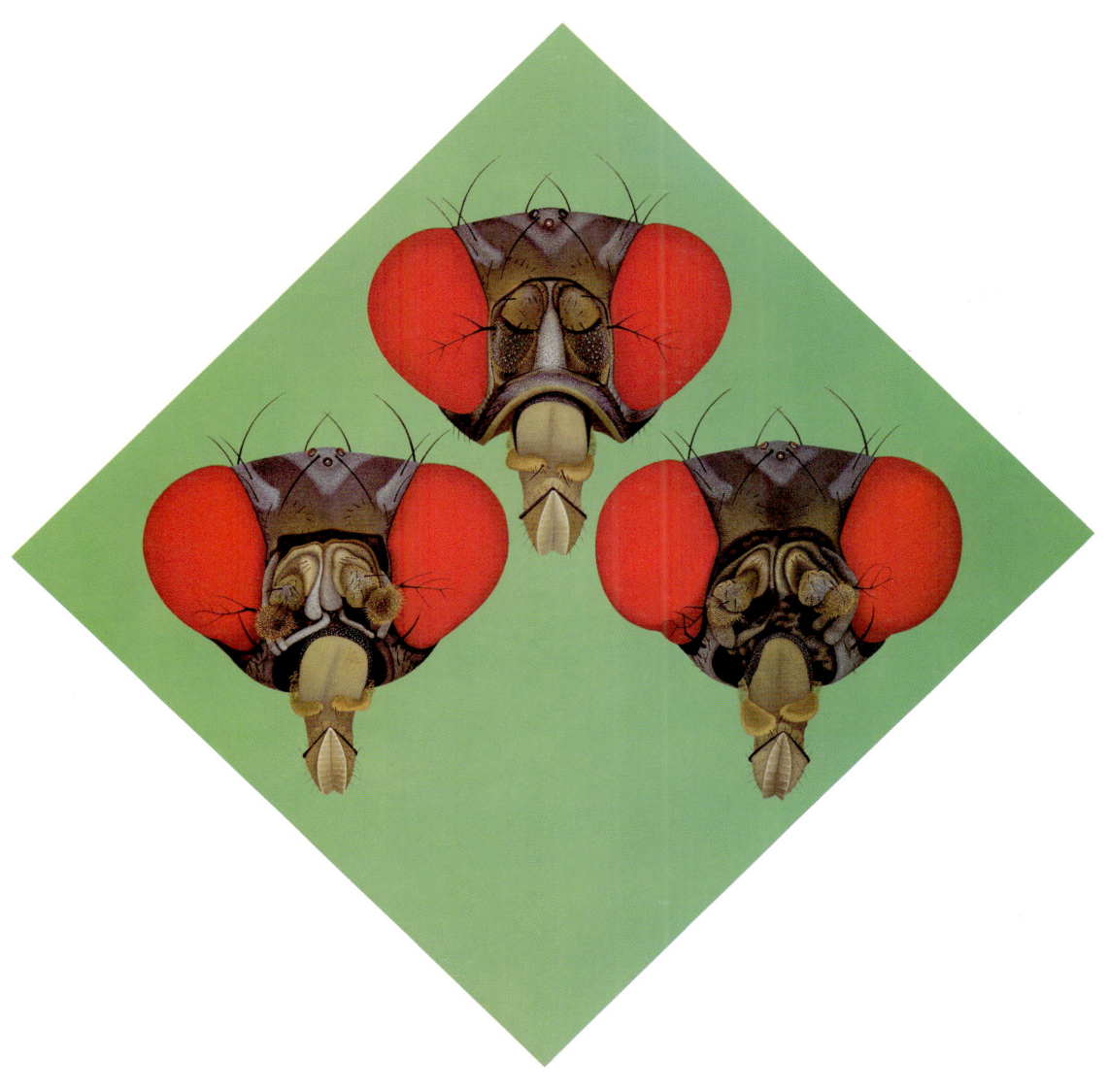

Laboratory flies, heads.
Varying deformations of Drosophila subobscura mutation - 'quasimodo'.
Top: healthy fly. Bottom left: hare-lip. Bottom right: wolf-throat.
University of Zürich.
1967. 40cm x 40cm.

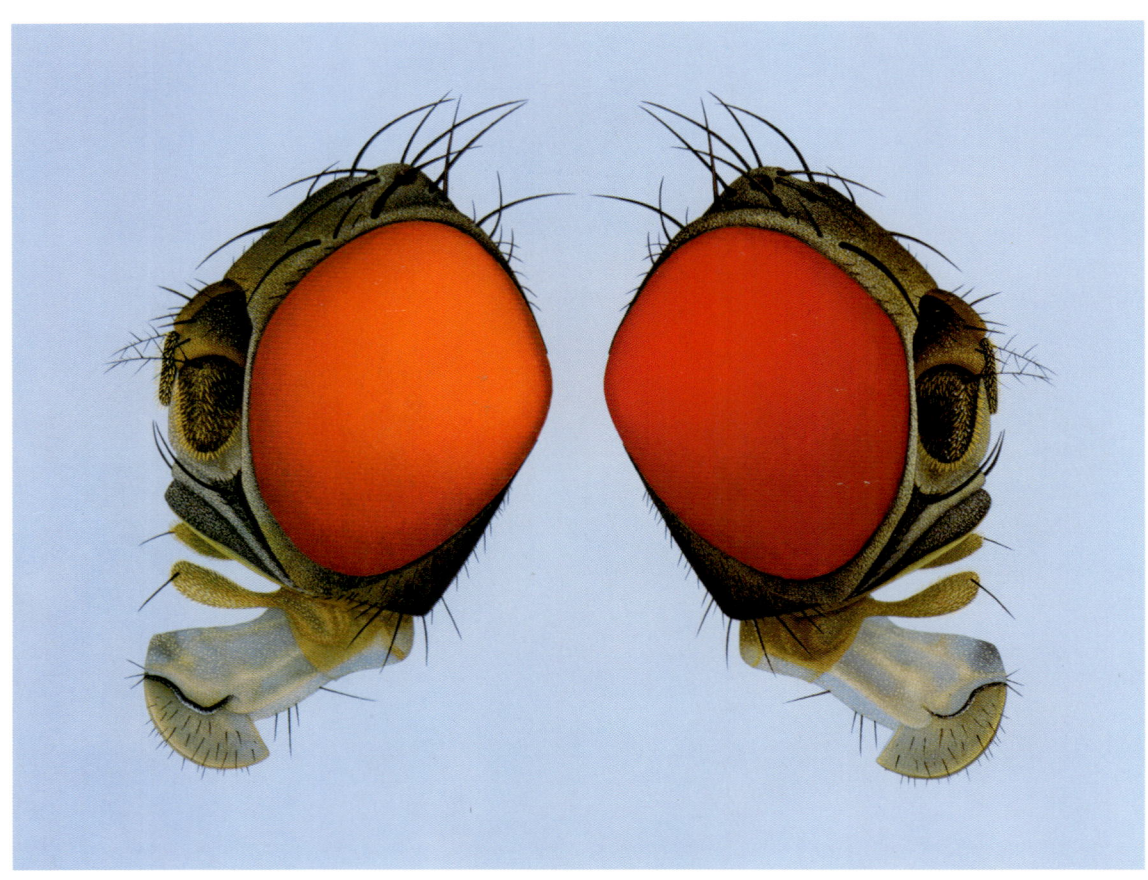

Laboratory flies, heads.
Left: mutated fly, orange eye. Right: healthy fly.
University of Zürich.
1968. 25cm x 30cm.

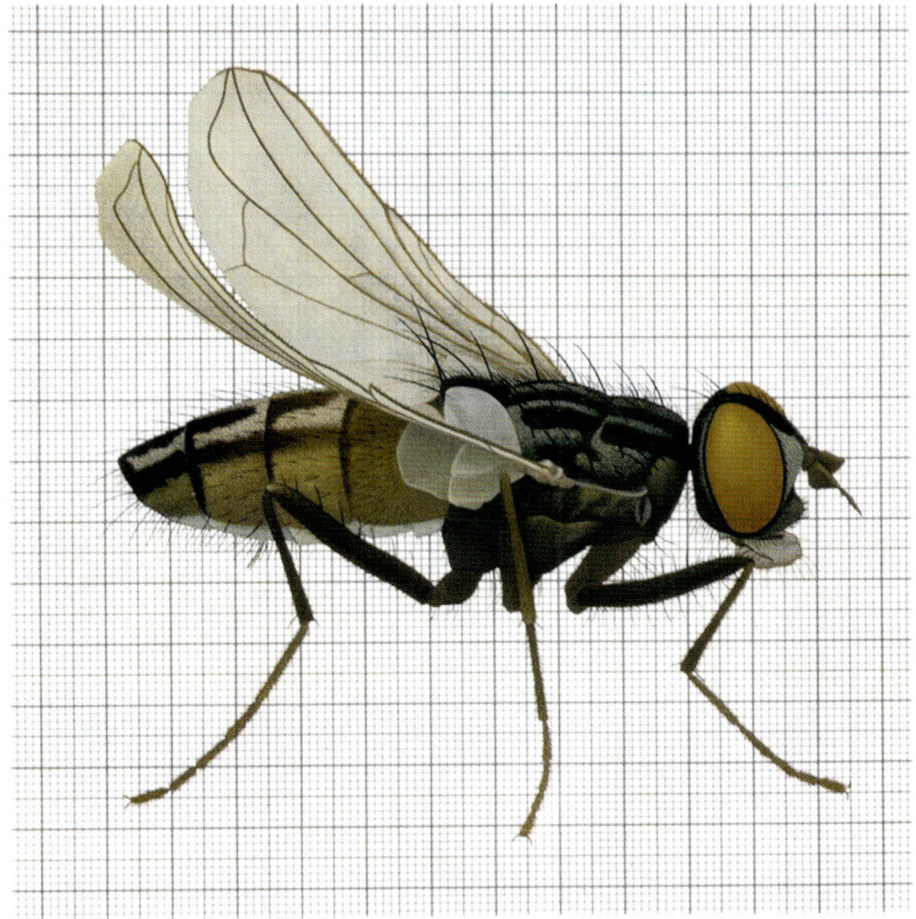

House fly (Mosca domestica mutation - 'aristapedia').
Fly mutated by x-rays at the Zoological Institute at the University of Zürich. Part of legs grow out of the feelers, the wings are bent
and no longer transparent, the eyes and body are yellow. In addition the chitin armour is much more brittle than that of wild flies.
Painted in Zürich at the time of the Chernobyl disaster.
University of Zürich.
1985-86. 44cm x 54.8cm.

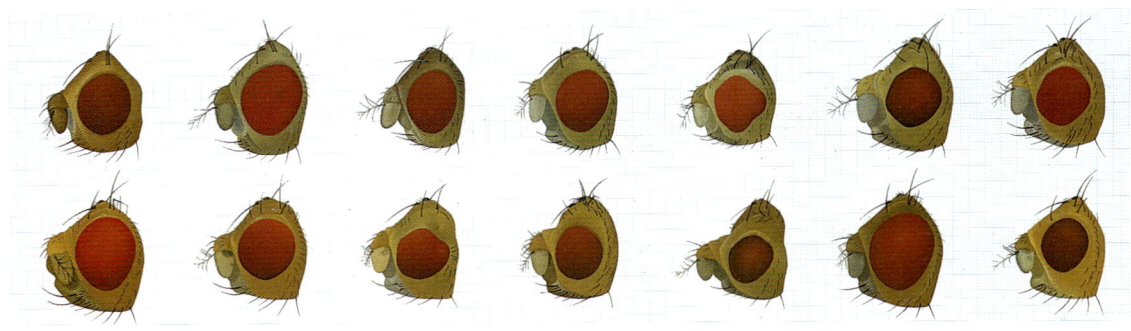

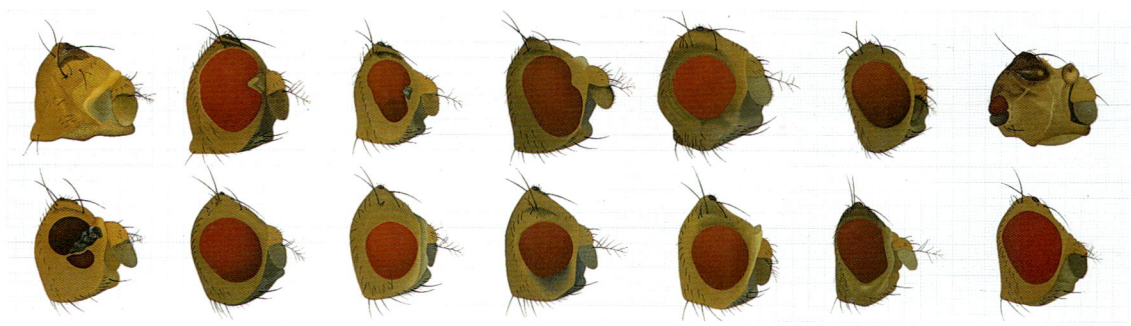

Flies (Drosophila melanogaster) mutated by x-rays at the Zoological Institute at the University of Zürich.
Top: ey - IID. Deformed heads and eyes. 1986.
Bottom: ey-opt. Wings growing out of the eyes. 1986-87.
Painted in Zürich.
University of Zürich.
Each picture: 29cm x 21cm.

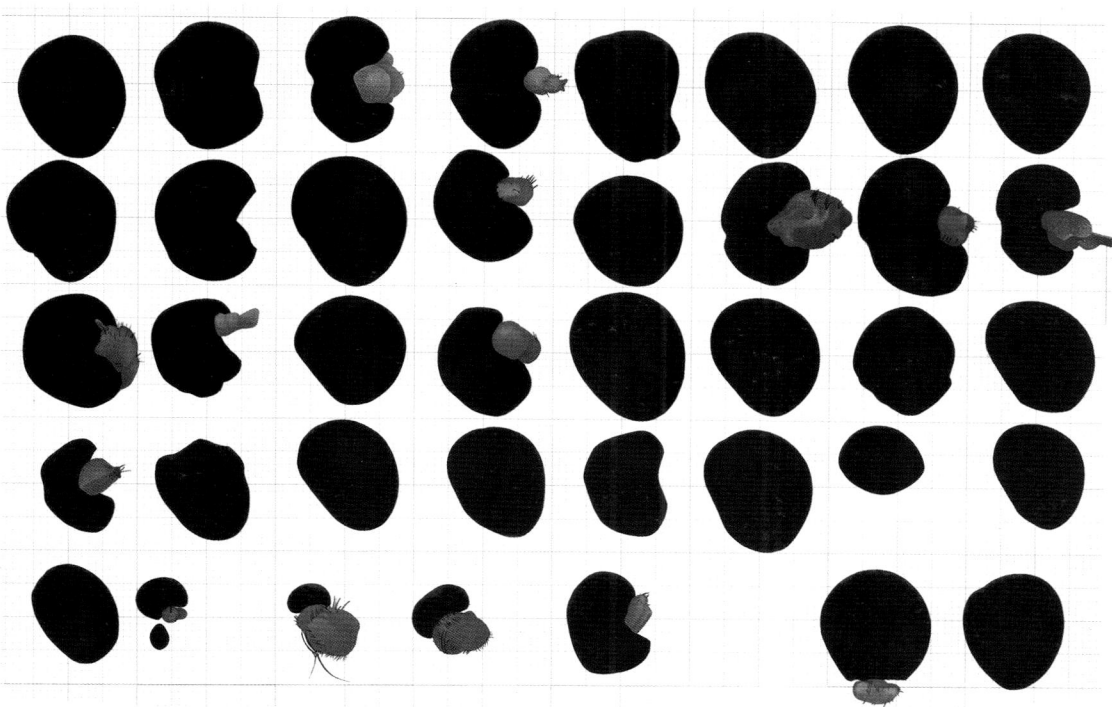

Flies (Drosophila melanogaster) mutated by x-rays at the Zoological Institute at the University of Zürich.
Eyes painted black instead of red.
Painted in Zürich.
University of Zürich.
1986-87. 40cm x 54.5cm.

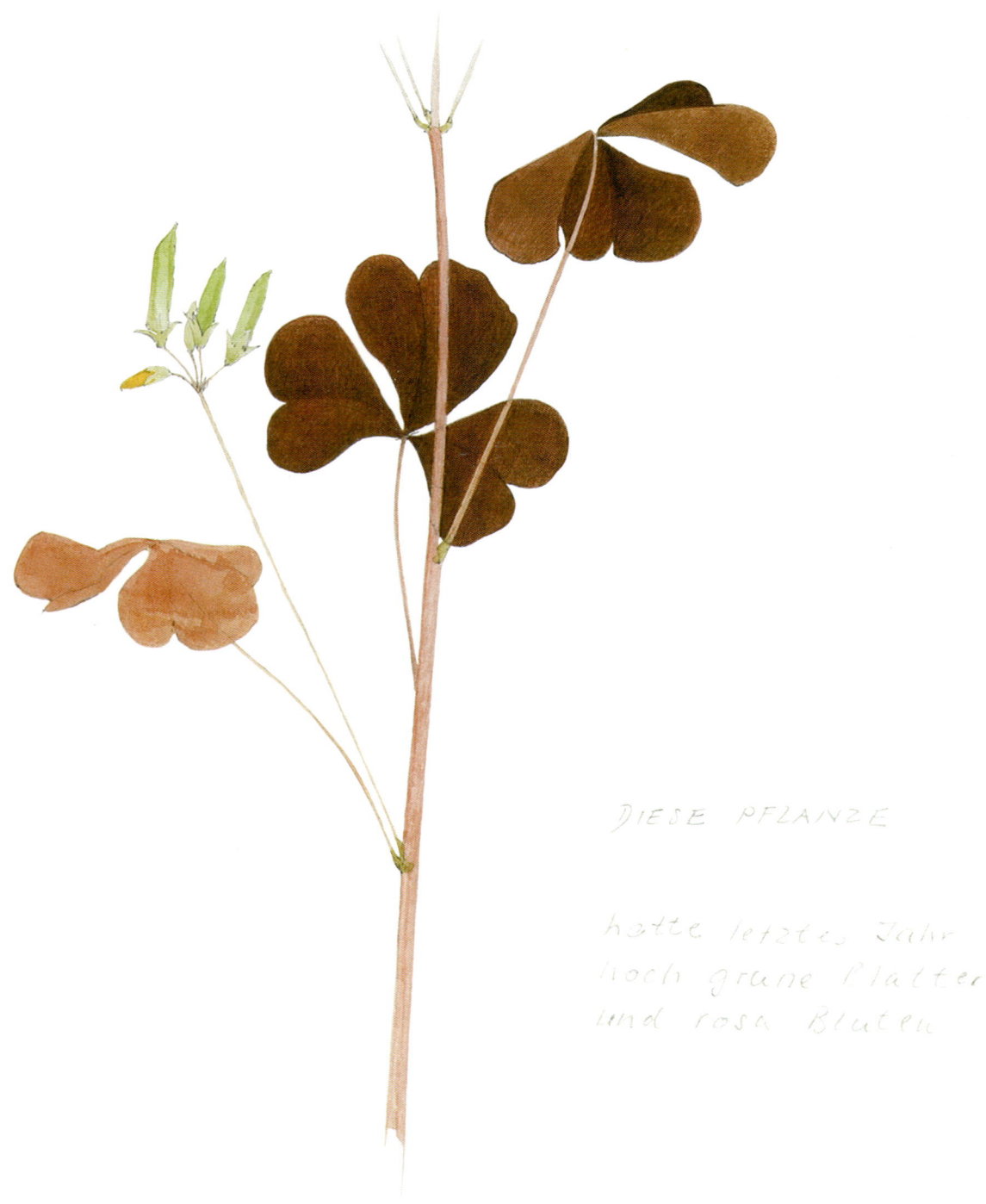

DIESE PFLANZE

hatte letztes Jahr
noch grüne Blätter
und rosa Blüten

Clover.
Clover is red instead of green, flower is yellow instead of pink.
Found in Gysinge.
1987. 29.7cm x 21cm.

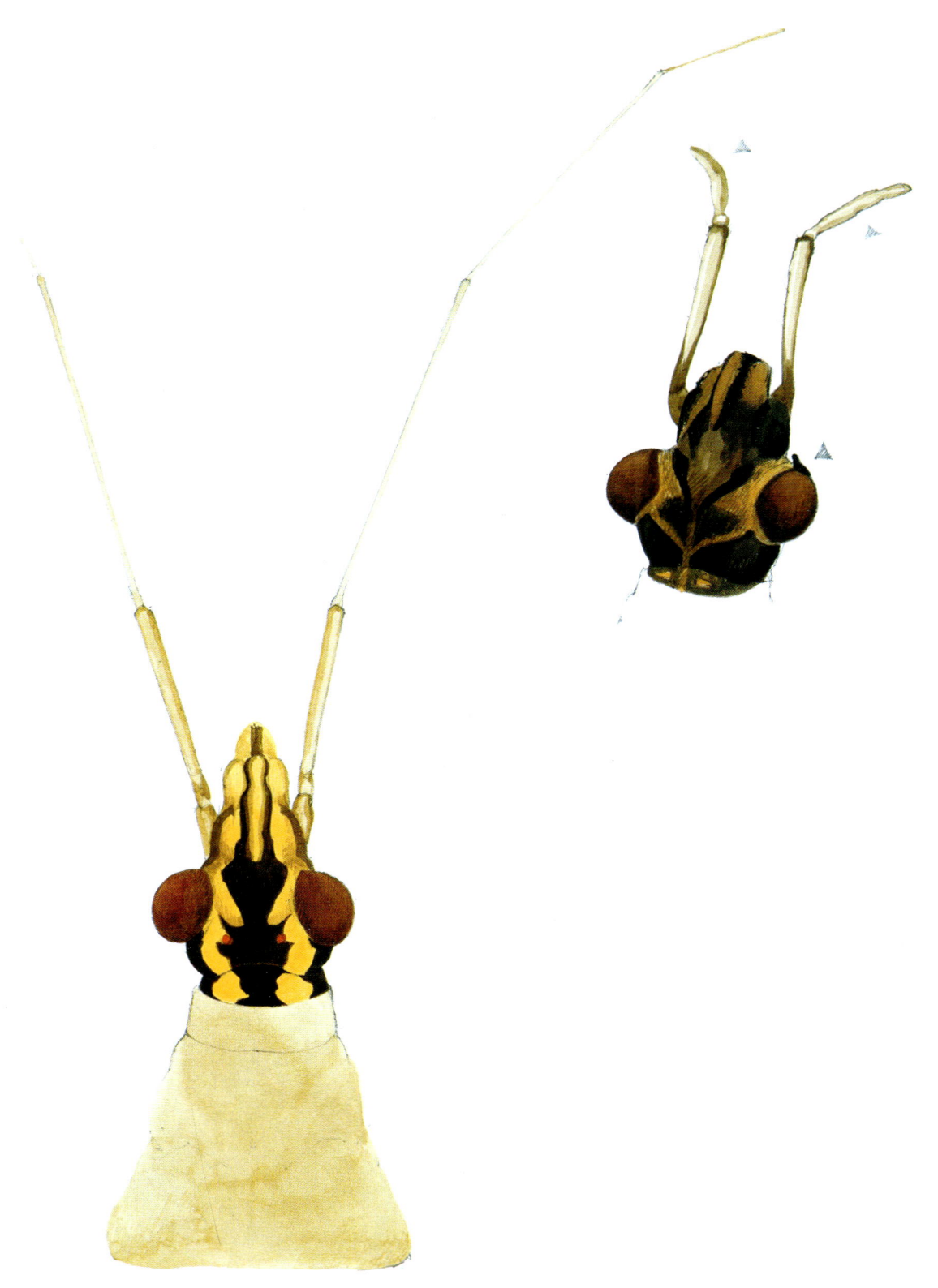

Two damsel bugs, heads (Nabis rugosus).
Below left: healthy head.
Above right: shortened feelers and black growth out of right eye.
Found and painted in Gysinge.
1987. 29.7cm x 21cm.

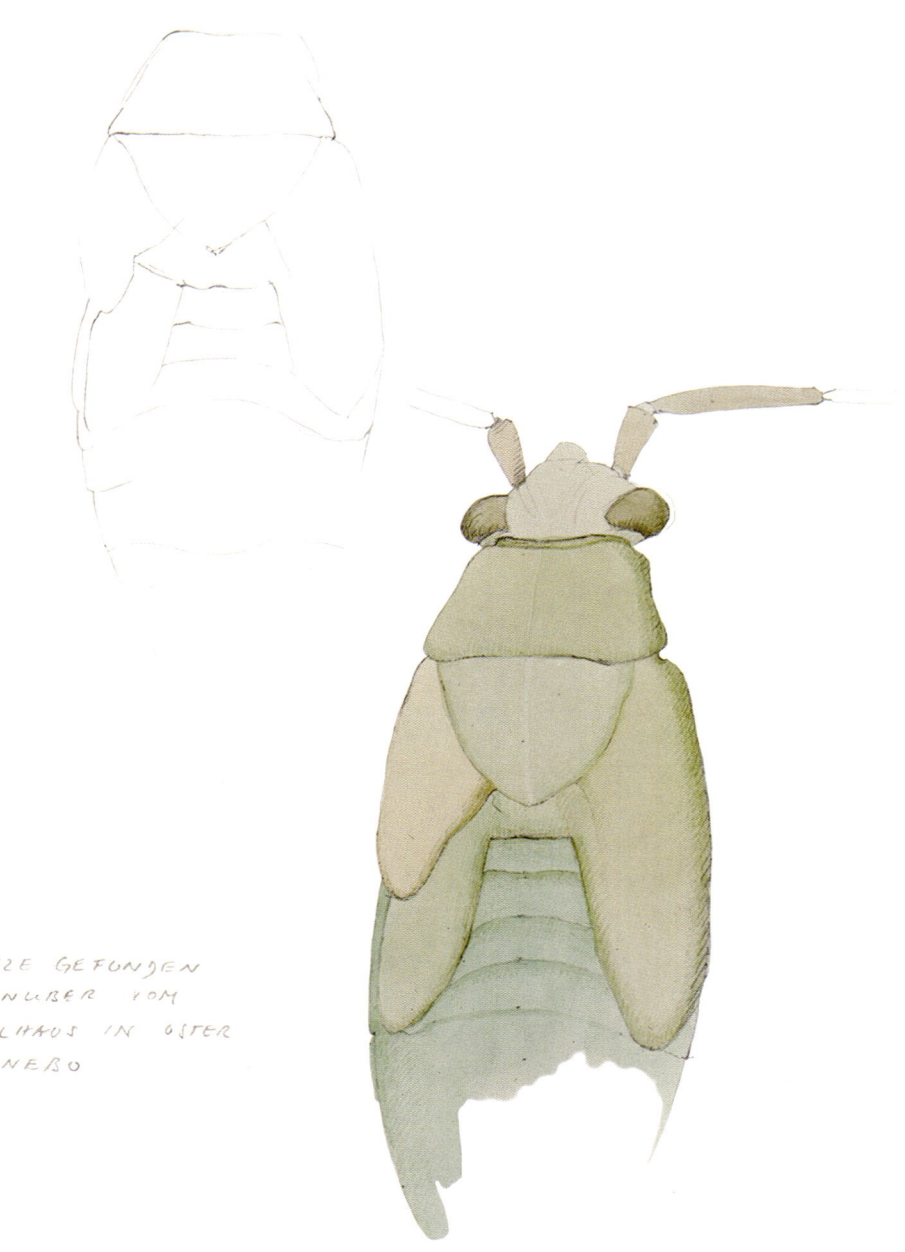

WANZE GEFUNDEN
GEGENUBER VOM
SCHULHAUS IN OSTER
FÄRNEBO

L. Hesse. Howith

Gysinge 31. Jul. 87

Soft bug, larva (Deraeocoris ruber).
The left pair of wings is divided in the upper and lower wing. Found in Österfärnebo. Painted in Gysinge.
1987. 29.7cm x 21cm.

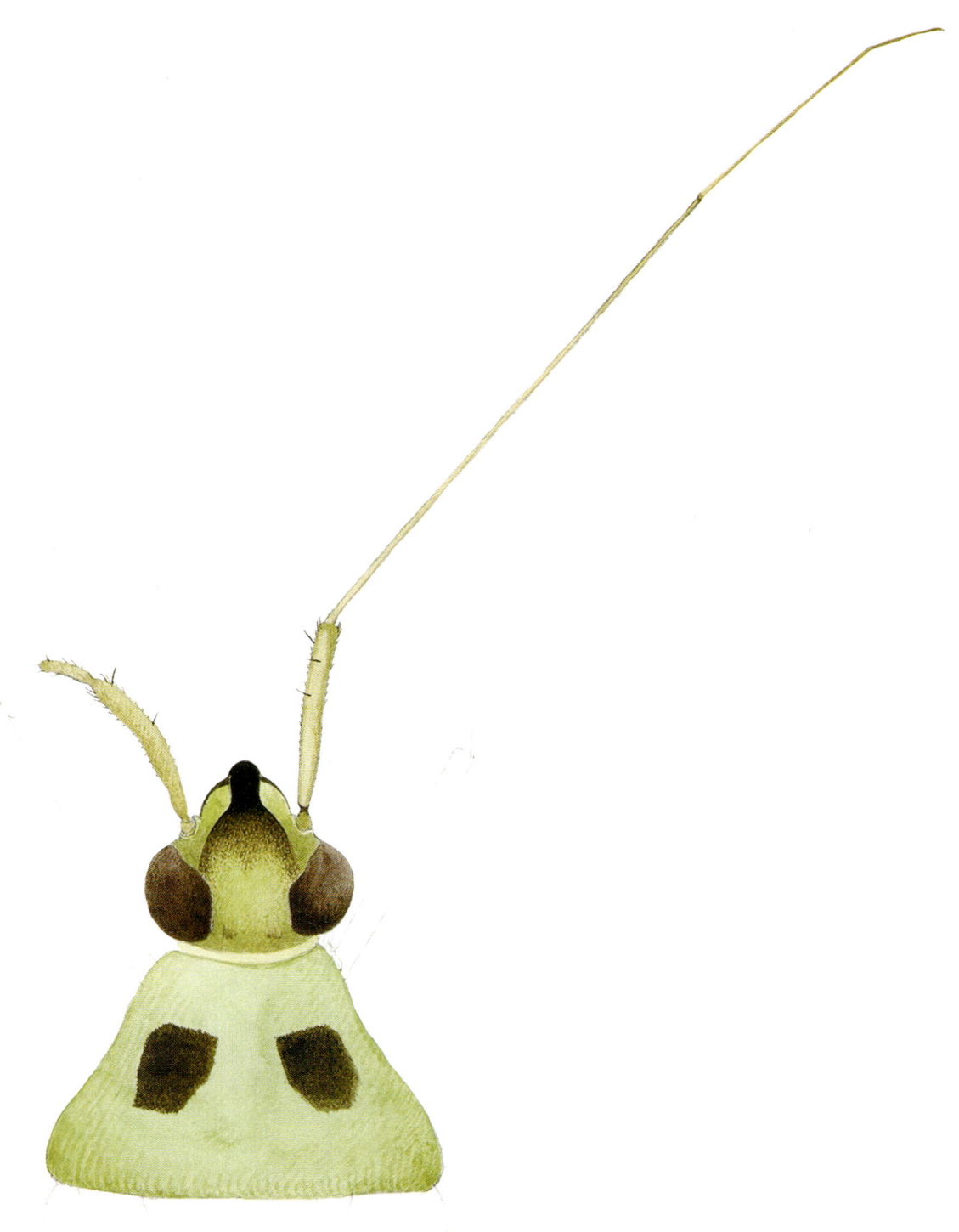

Soft bug, feeler (Miridae).
Left feeler: deformed. Right feeler: normal.
Found in Gävle. Painted in Gysinge
1987. 29.7cm x 21cm.

TICINO

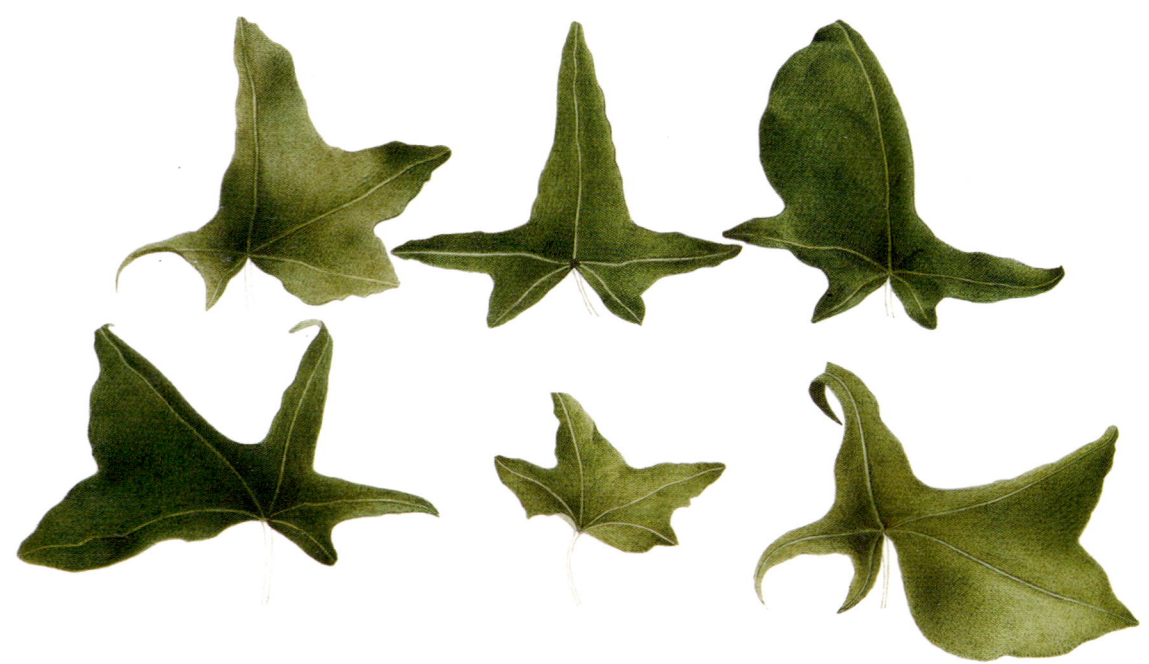

Ivy leaves.
Found in Mendrisio. Painted in Zürich.
Collection of Graphische Sammlung ETH Zürich.
1987. 29.7cm x 21cm.

Farbskizze eines narkotisierten Drosophila melanogaster Männchens

Ausser dem linken Flügel ist alles normal

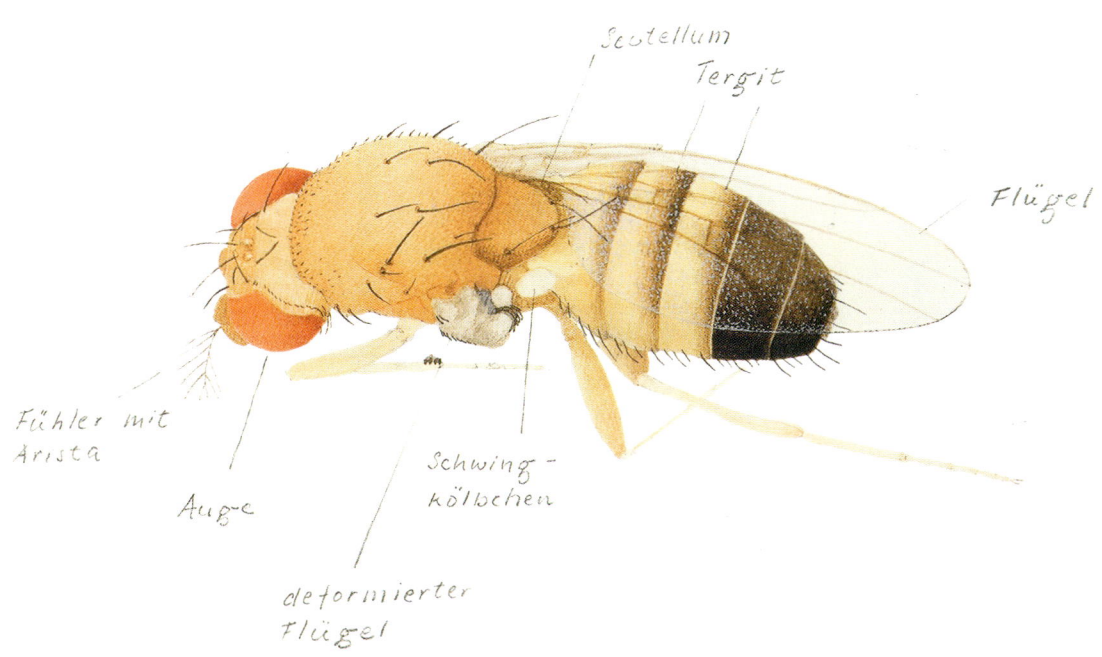

Scotellum

Tergit

Flügel

Fühler mit
Arista

Auge

Schwing-
kölbchen

deformierter
Flügel

Bred fly (Drosophila melanogaster).
Offspring of parents found in Rancate. Painted in Zürich.
The fly has a clubbed wing. The right, normal wing stretches over the back of the body
1987. 29.7cm x 21cm.

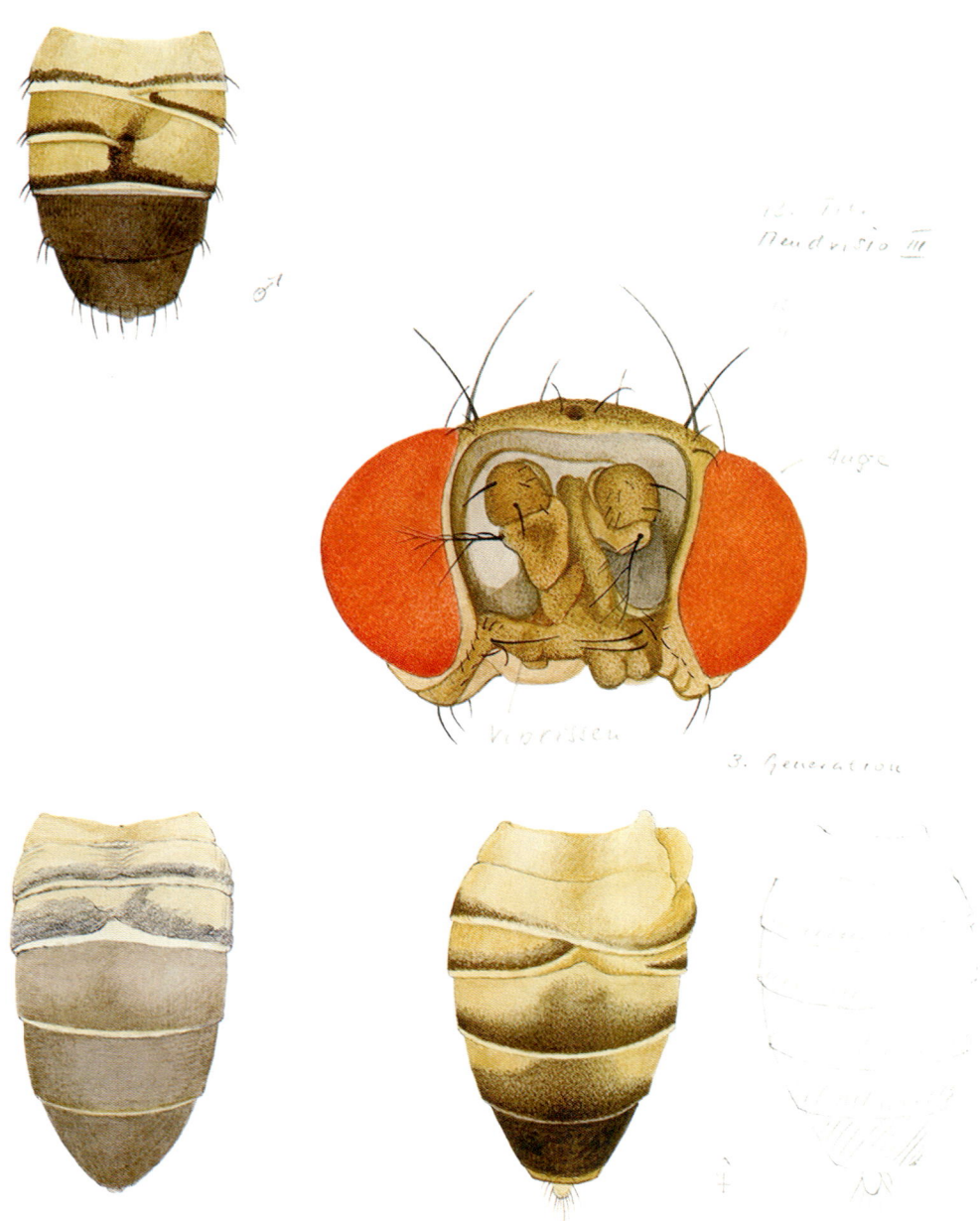

Abdomens and head (third Generation Mendrisio III).
Three abdomens with disturbed segments of the abdomen. The head shows eyes with different shapes, disturbed feelers, bent vibrissae and split carina.
Painted in Zürich.
1987. 29.7cm x 21cm.

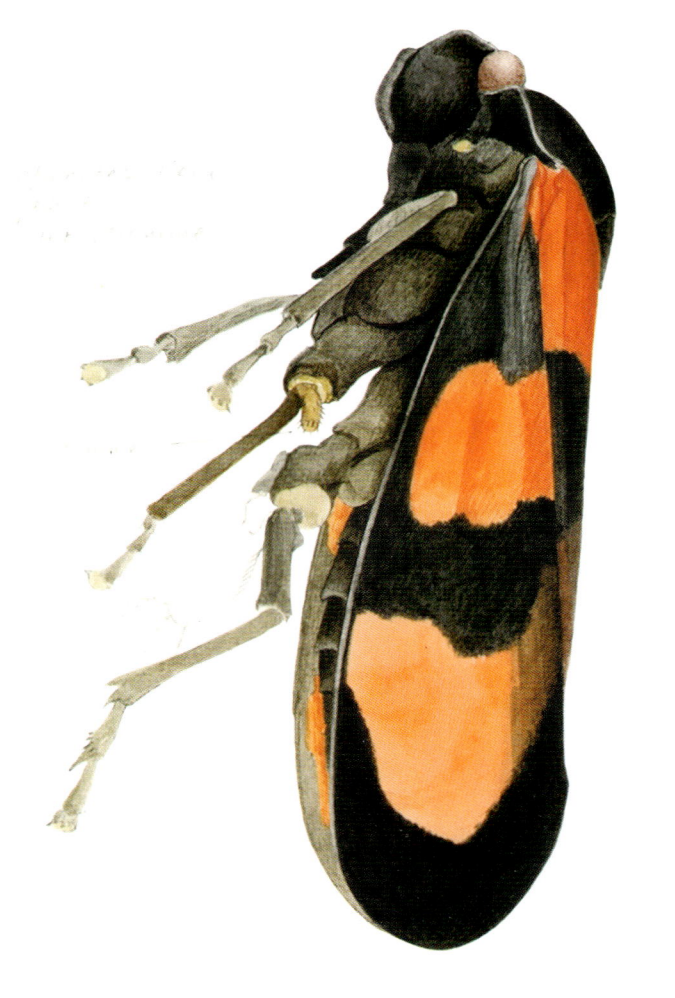

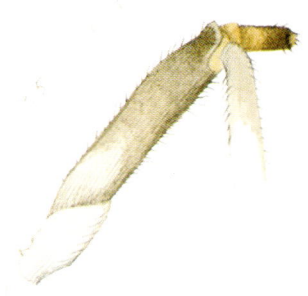

Leaf hopper.
Part of leg growing out of the middle leg. Found in Rancate.
Painted in Zürich.
Collection of Graphische Sammlung ETH Zürich.
1988. 42cm x 29.7cm.

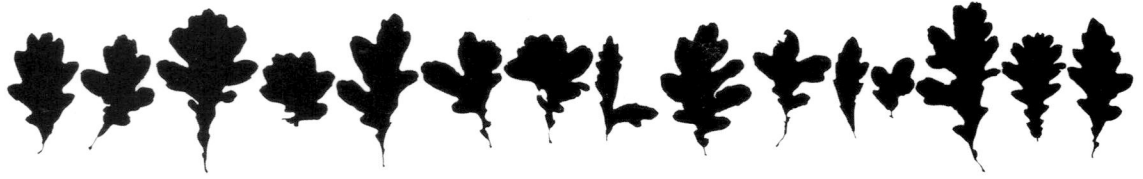

Oak leaves.
Found near Leibstadt, Canton of Aargau.
1989. 21cm x 94cm.

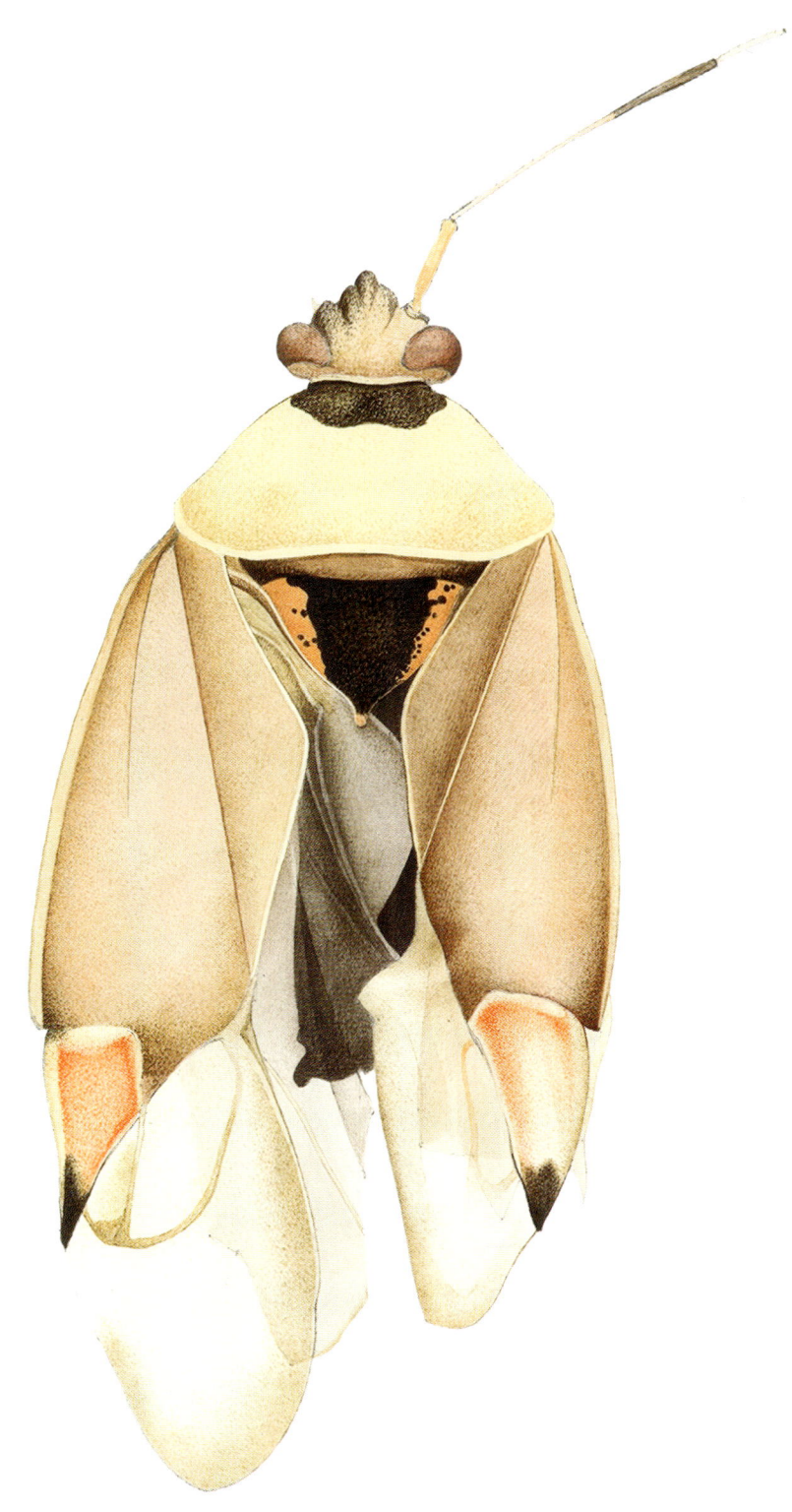

Soft bug, wings (Deraeocoris ruber).
The right wing is too short. The short feeler has no deformation (it broke off).
Found near the Gösgen power plant. Painted in Zürich
1988. 29.7cm x 21cm.

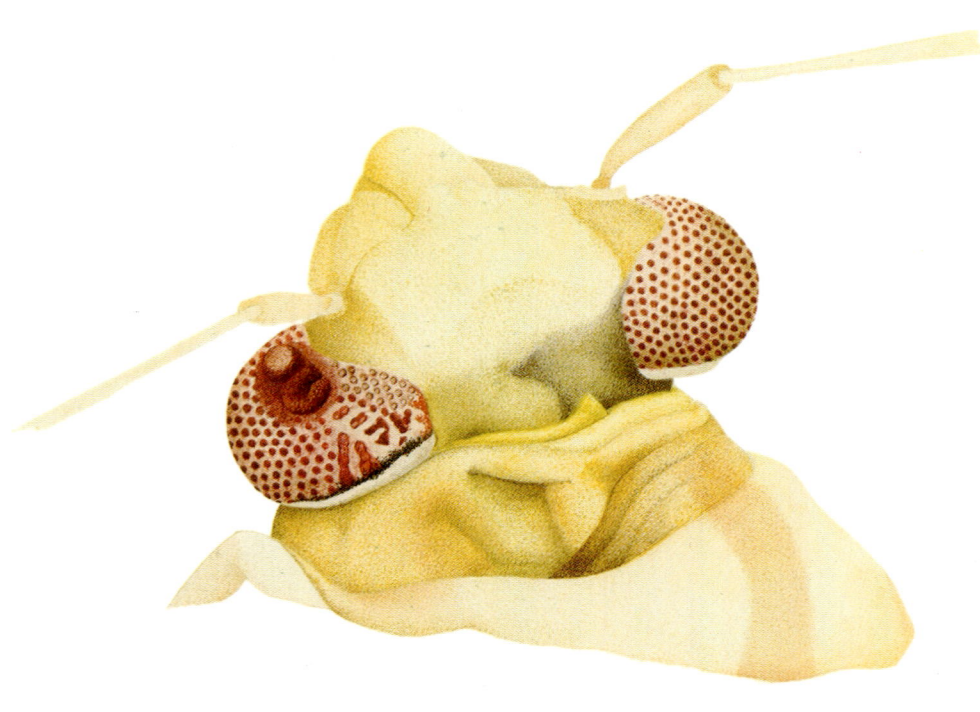

Head of soft bug larva (Miridae).
Irregular facets on left eye and a growth in the colour of the eye.
Found near the Gösgen power plant. Painted in Zürich.
1988. 29.7cm x 21cm.

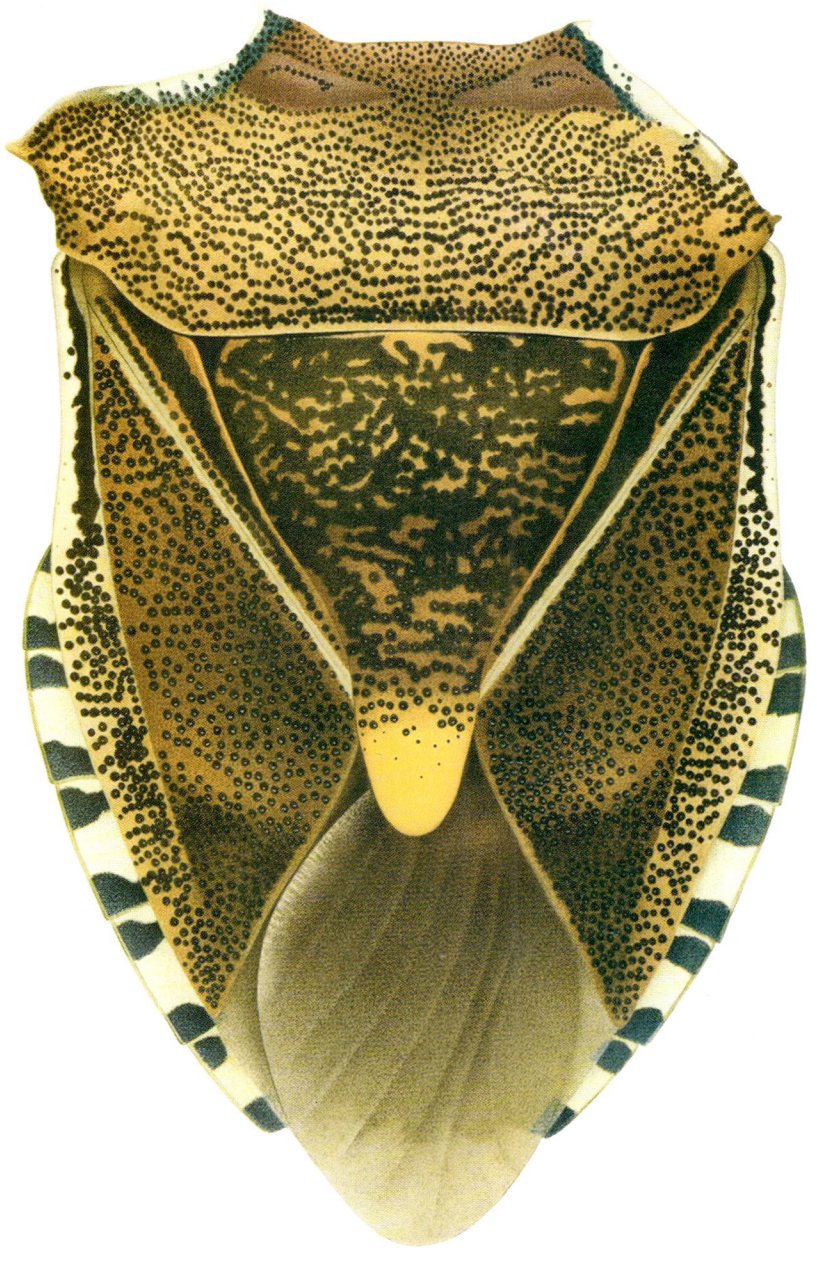

Tree bug (Pentatomidae rufipes).
Neck plate on right side without point.
Found in area of Paul Scherrer Institute (by J.Jenny). Painted in Zürich.
Collection of the Bundesamt für Kultur ‚Bern.
1992. 42cm x 29.7 cm.

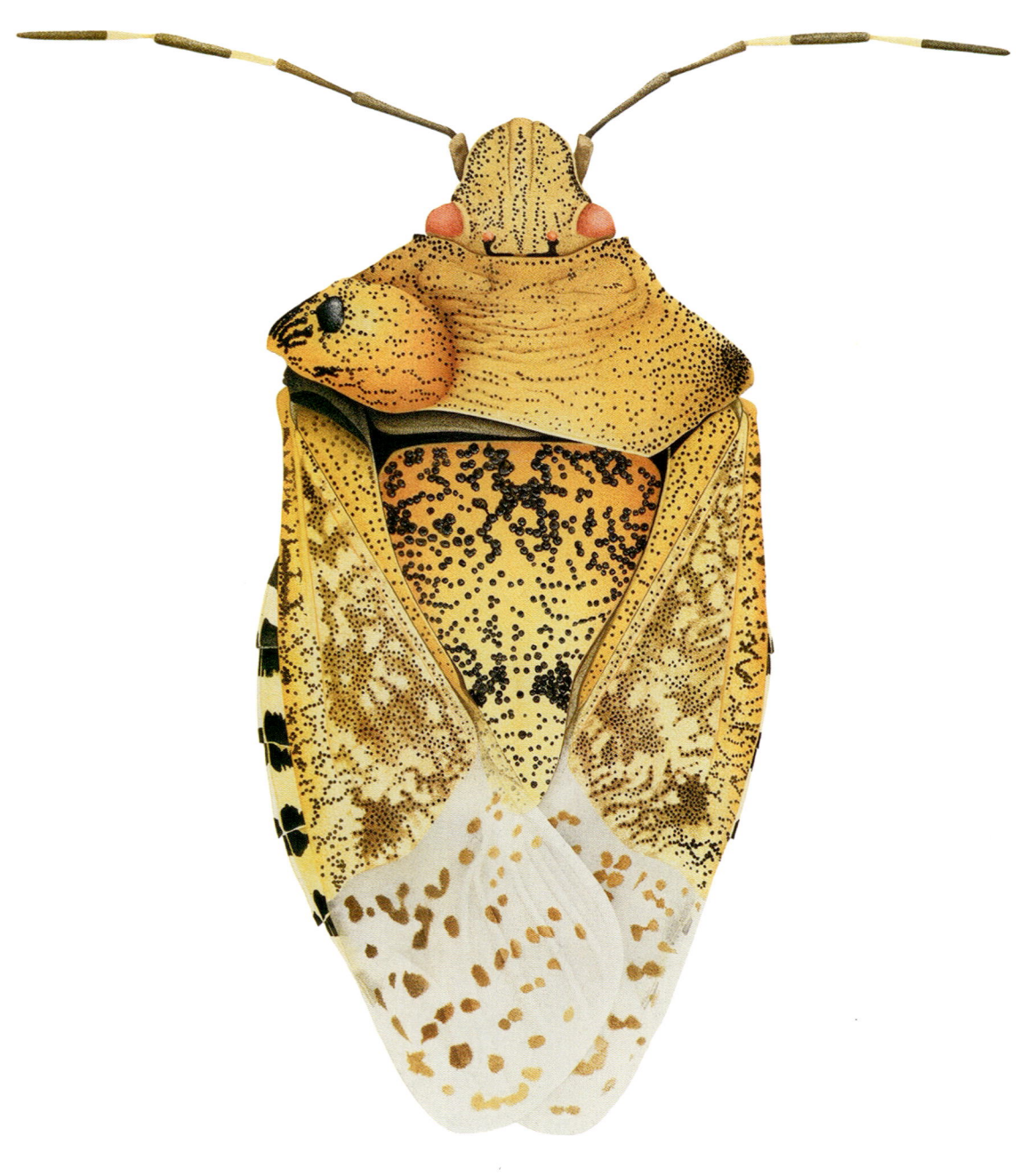

Garden bug (Raphigaster nebulosa).
The blister with a black growth changes the whole shape of the neck plate.
Found near the Leibstadt power plant, Germany (by J.Jenny). Painted in Zürich.
1991. 42cm x 29.7 cm.

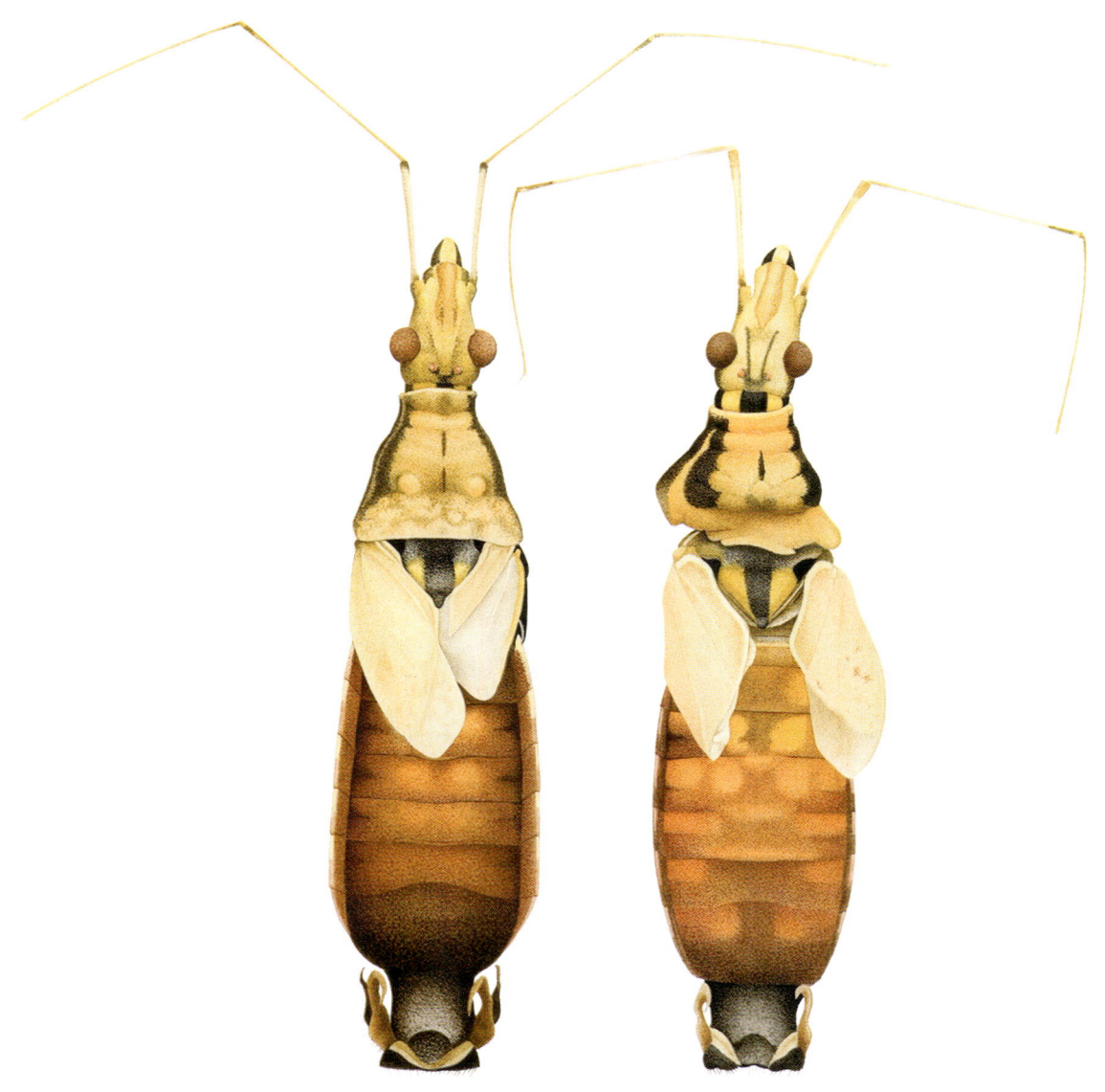

Two damsel bugs (Nabis rugosus).
Left: the right wing is too short.
Right: damaged wing as well as completely displaced and misshapen neck plate.
Found in the grounds of the Paul Scherrer Institure ETH (by J.Jenny). Painted in Zürich
1990-91. 42cm x 29.7cm.

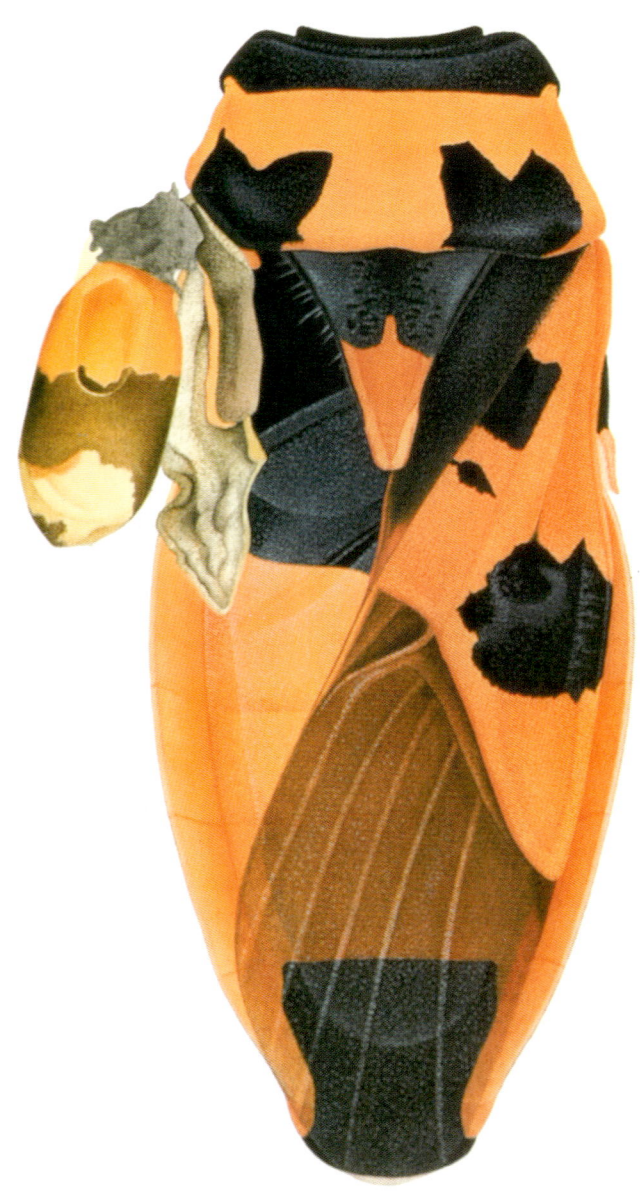

Glasswing bug (Corizus hyoscyami).
Left wing cover is short and balloon shaped. The otherwise flat underlying transparent wing is wavy and brownish.
Found in Würenlingen near the Paul Scherrer Institute ETH. Painted in Zürich
1988-89. 42cm x 29.7cm.

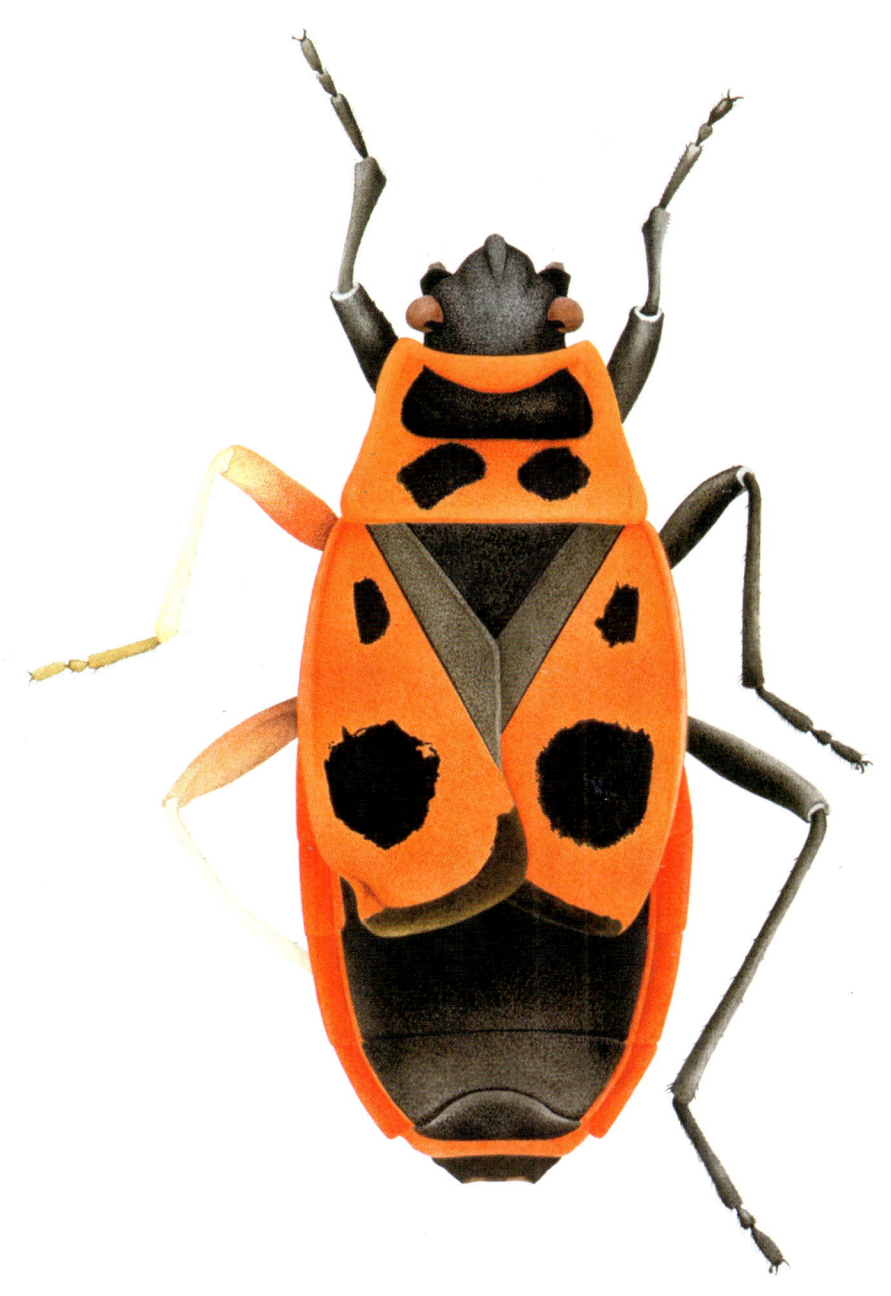

Fire bug, legs (Pyrrhocoris apterus).
Two legs on the left side are light and bent. The chitin armour is soft rather than firm.
Found in Bernau, near the Leibstadt power plant (by J.Jenny). Painted in Zürich.
1990. 42cm x 29.7 cm.

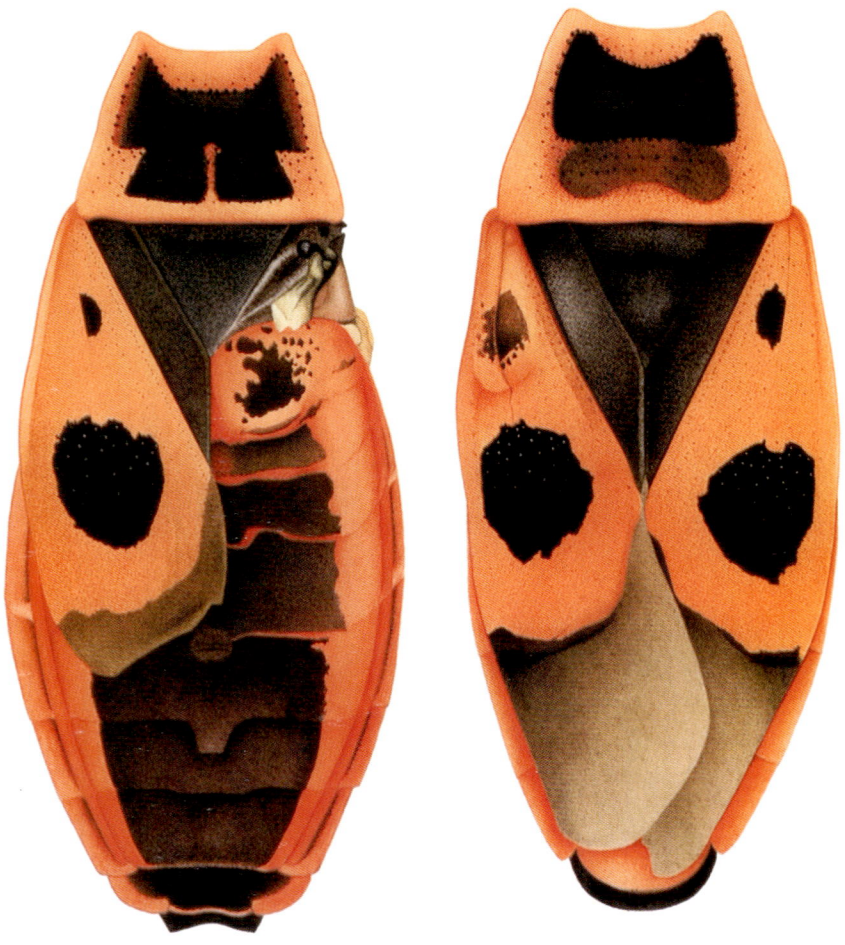

Two fire bugs (Pyrrhocoris apterus).
1. Generation bred in laboratory with food from Bernau.
Left: lacking the right cover wing. The small wing underneath has a blister. Right: blister on left wing.
The parents were found in Bernau, near the Leibstadt power plant ((by J.Jenny). Painted in Zürich.
1990. 42cm x 29.7 cm.

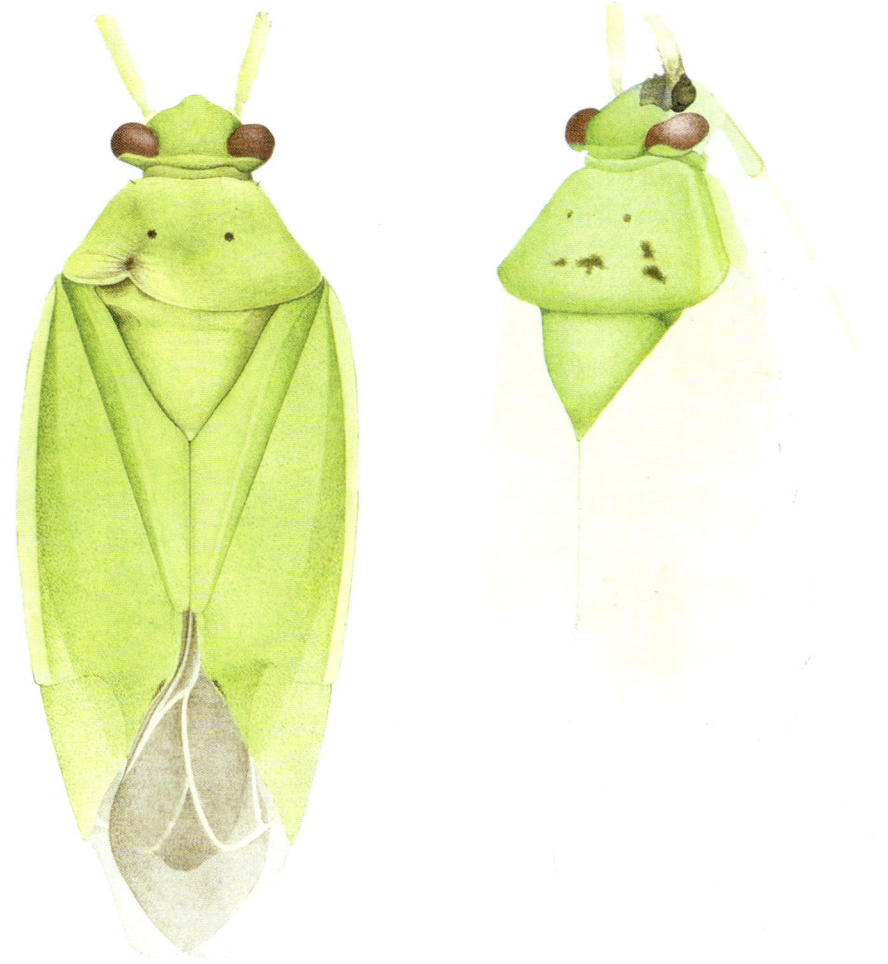

Two soft bugs (Miridae).
Left: dark patches and deformed neck plate. Found in Seascale. Painted in Holmrook.
Right: heavy growth on base of the right feeler and dark patches on neck plate. Found in Drigg. Painted in Holmrook.
1989. 42cm x 29.7cm.

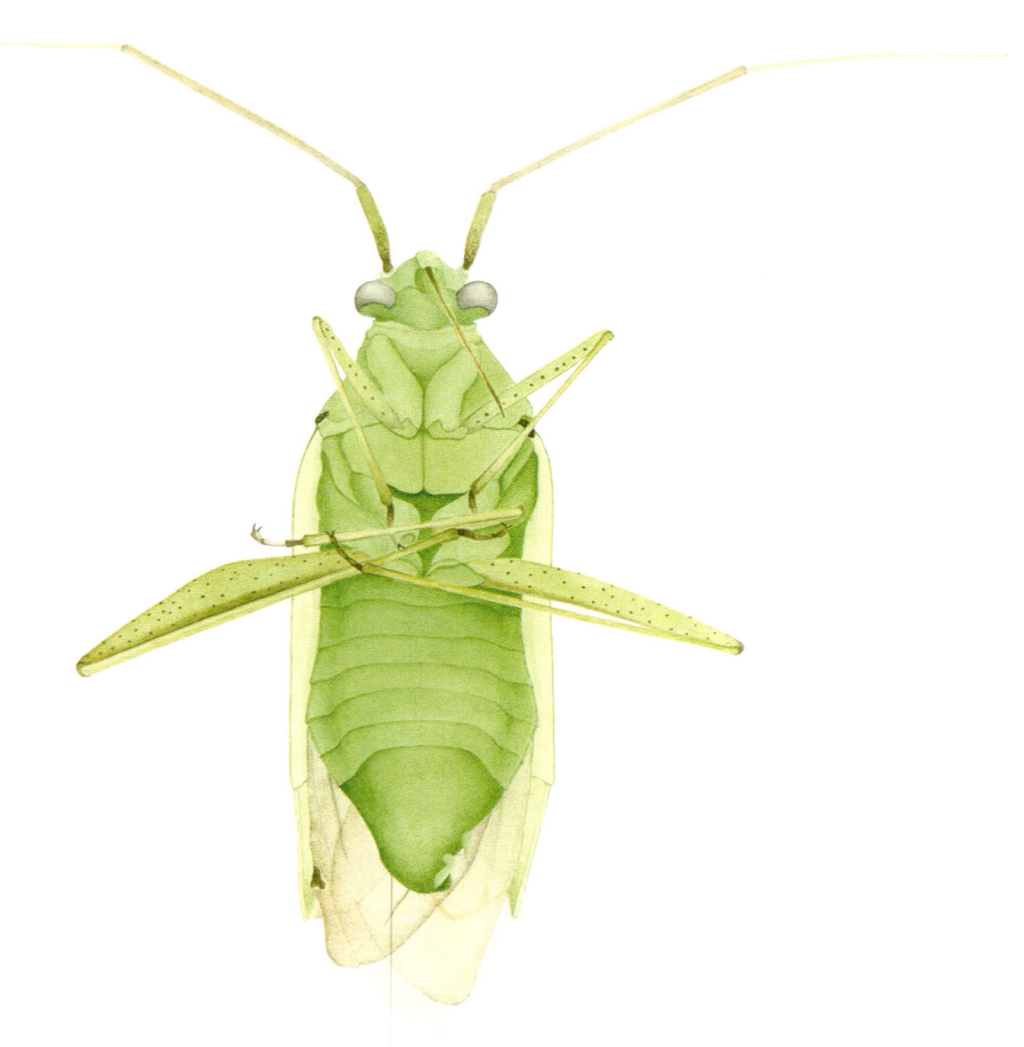

Soft bug, wing (Miridae).
Left wing is darker and thicker.
Found and painted in Seascale.
1989. 42cm x 29.7cm.

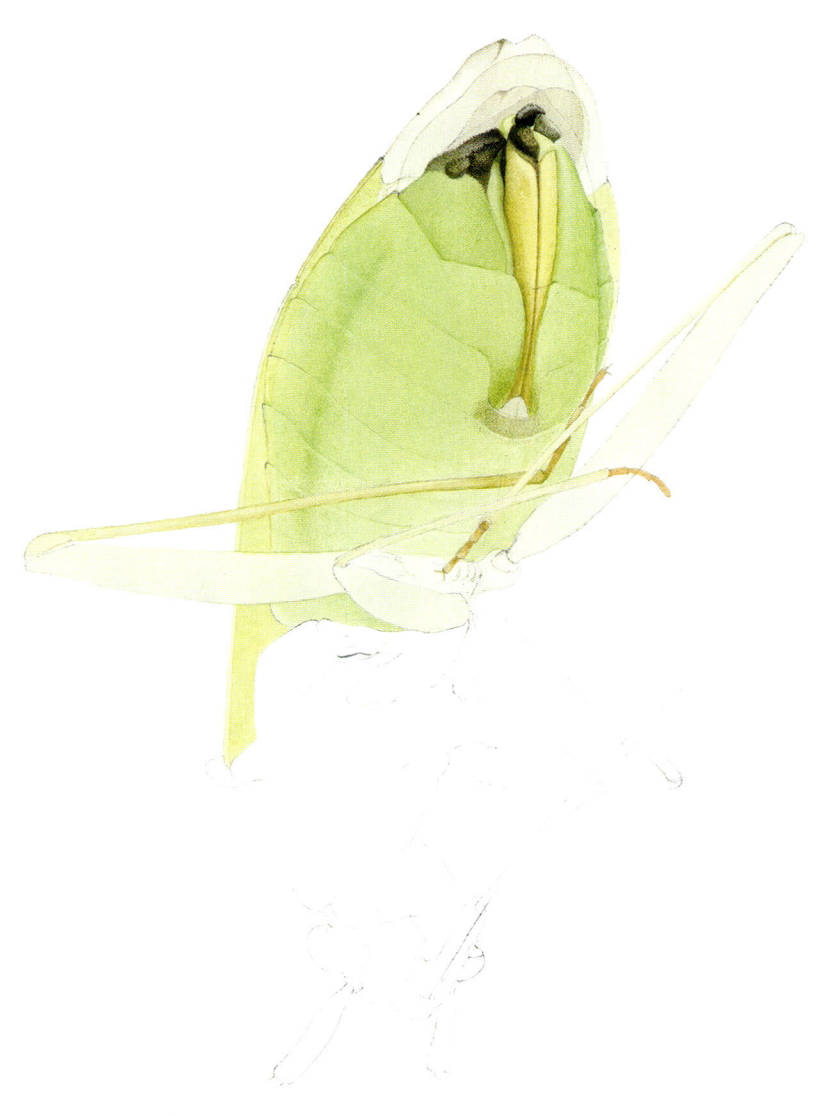

Soft bug (Miridae).
Heavy growth on the genitals.
Found and painted in Seascale.
1989. 42cm x 29.7cm

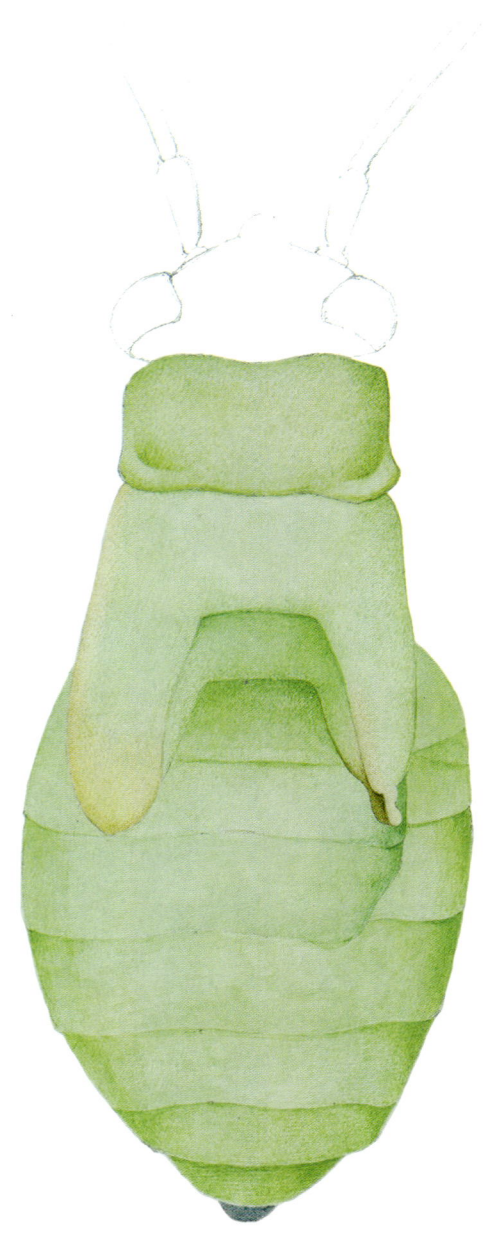

Soft bug larva (Miridae).
The wings on the right side are split and crumpled at the end.
Found in area near Ponsonby. Painted in Holmrook
1989. 42cm x 29.7cm.

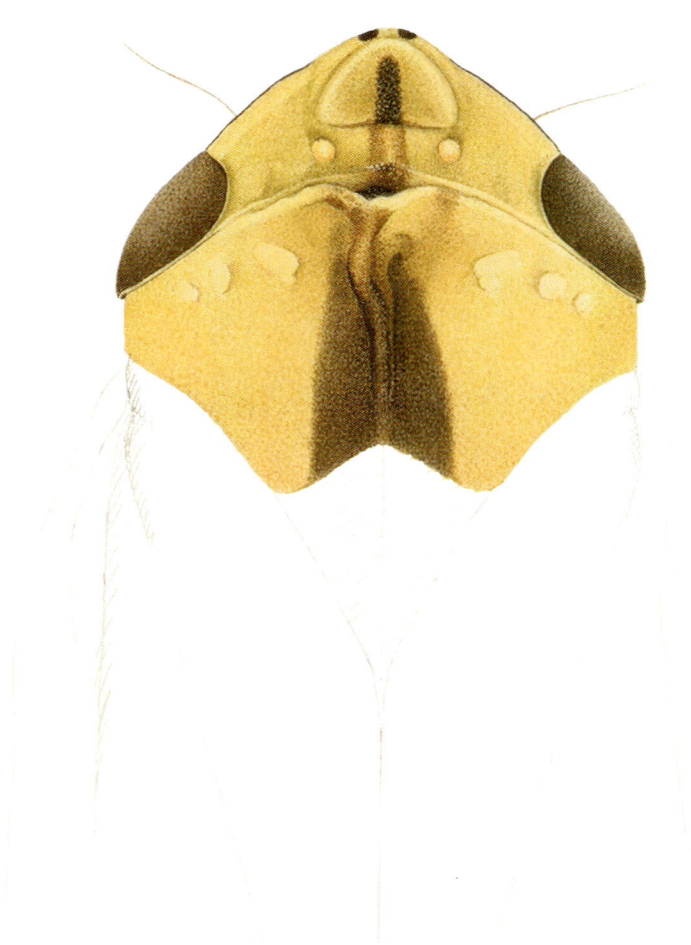

Head of a leaf hopper (Cicada).
The bent neckplate causes a hole to appear.
Found in area near Ponsonby. Painted in Zürich.
1989. 29.7cm x 42cm.

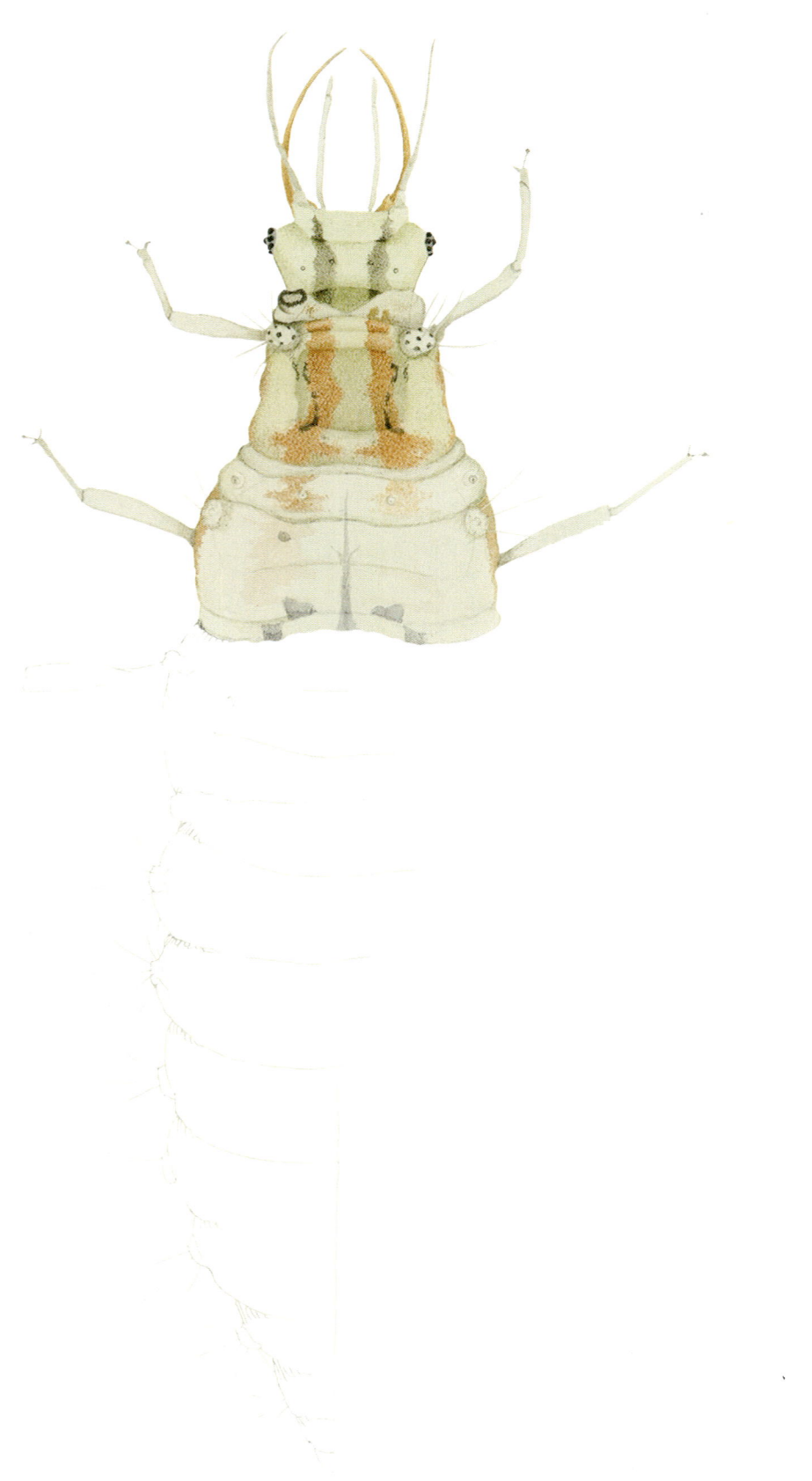

Unidentified larva.
Large hole with dark ring on the left shoulder.
Found in Ponsonby. Painted in Holmrook.
1989. 29.7cm x 21cm.

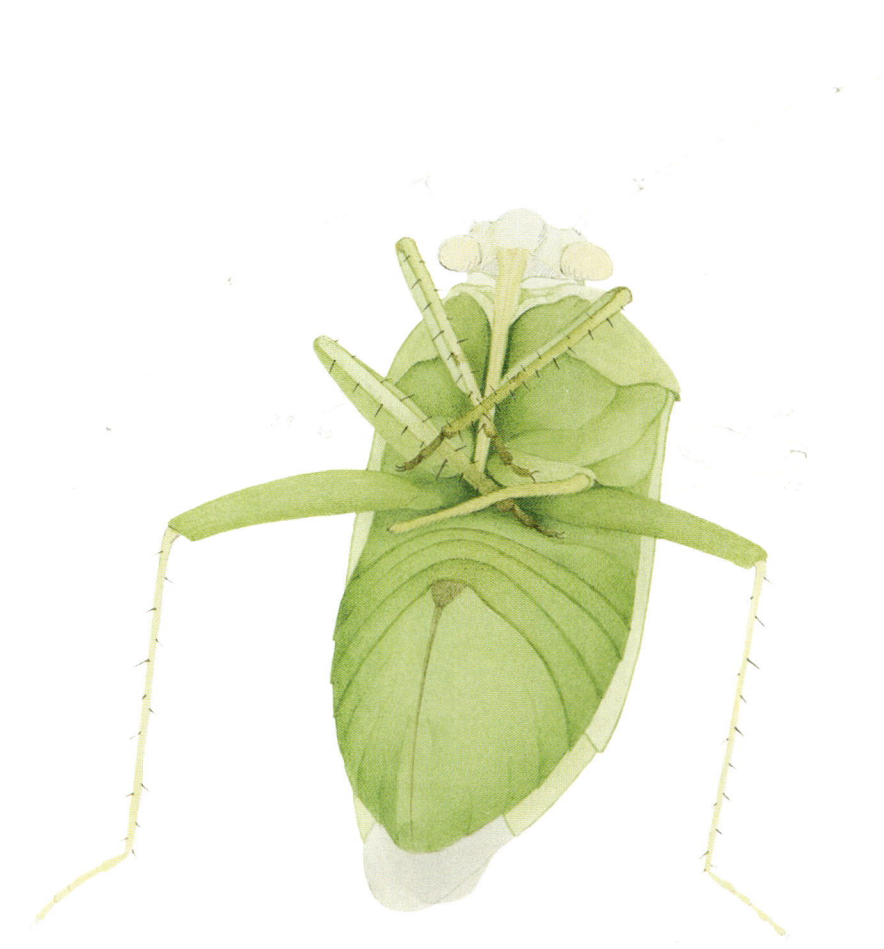

Soft bug (Miridae).
The middle leg is wavy, short and without foot, only with toes at the end of the leg.
Found in Pripjat, Ukraine. Painted in Kiev and Zürich
1990. 34cm x 24cm.

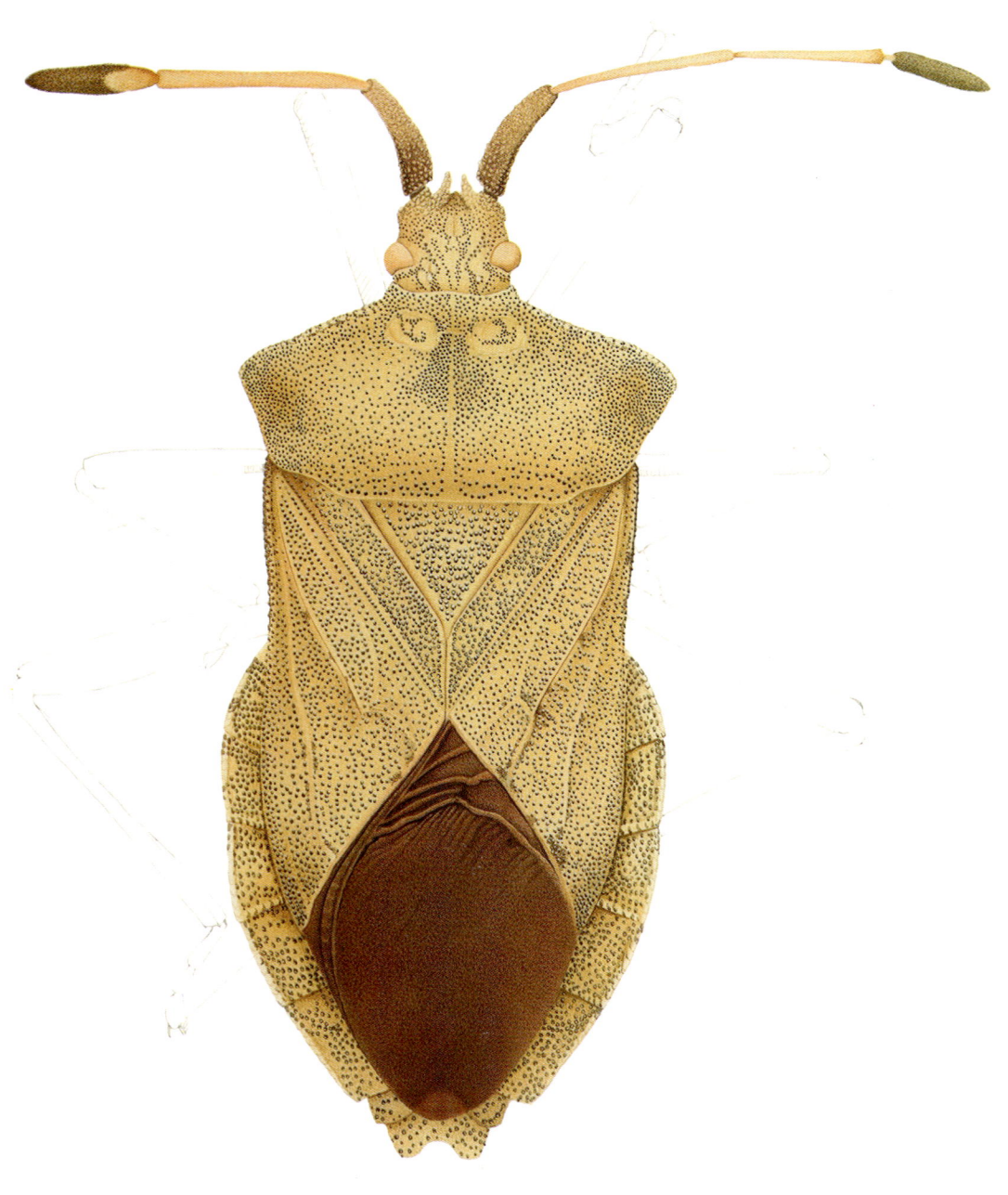

Squash bug, feeler (Coreidae).
Section of left feeler missing.
Found in Polesskoje, Ukraine. Painted in Zürich.
1990. 42cm x 29.7cm.

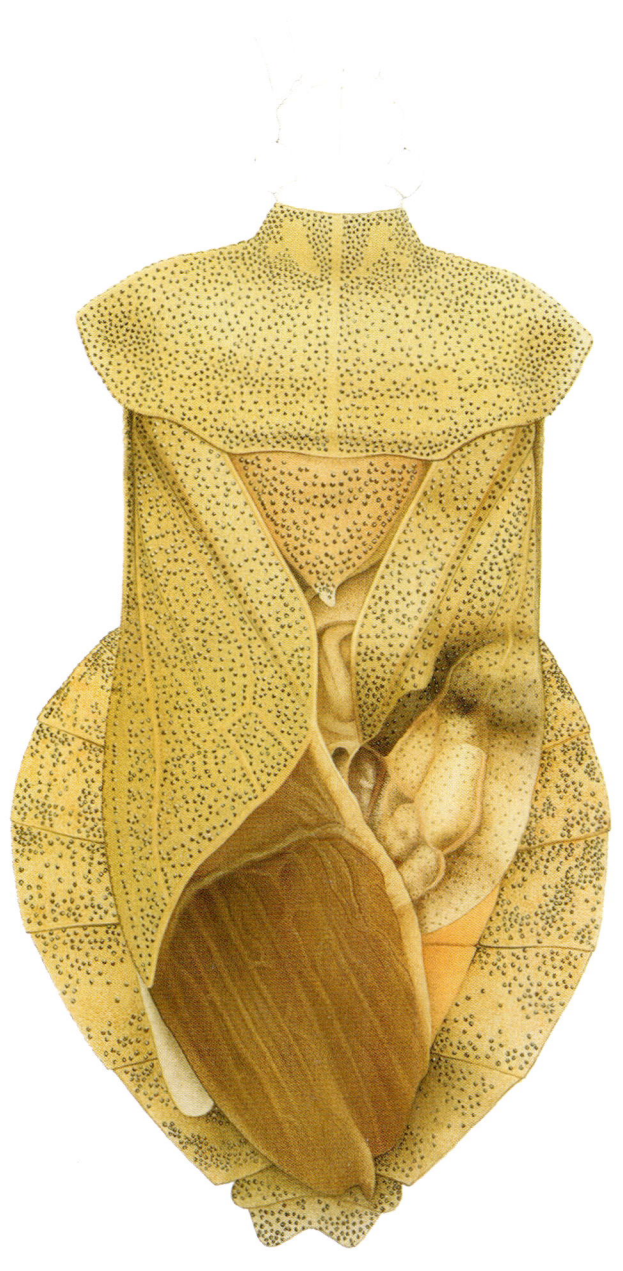

Squash bug, wing (Coreidae).
Bent wings, crumpled and too light in colour.
Found in Polesskoje, Ukraine. Painted in Zürich.
1990. 42cm x 29.7cm.

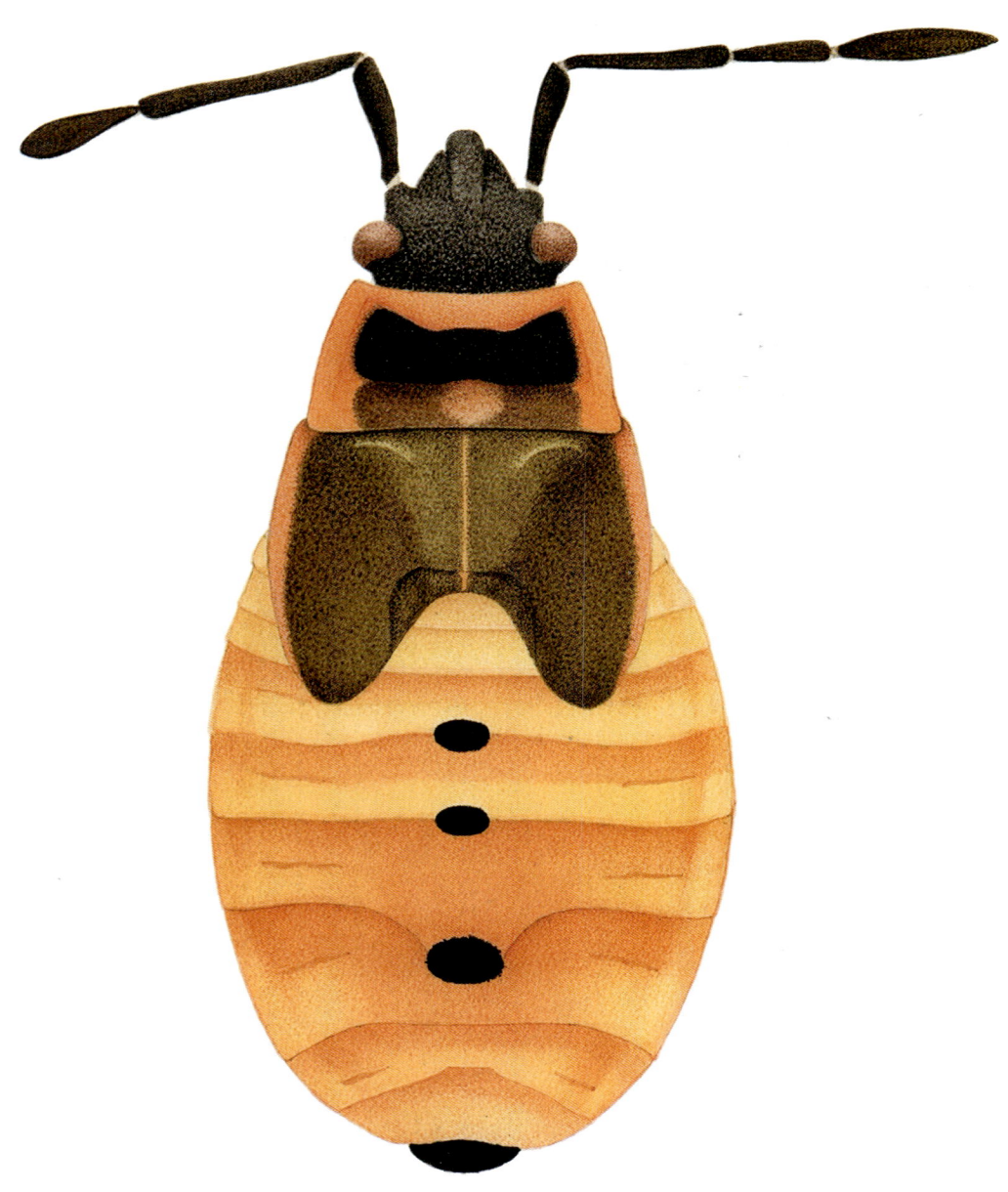

Fire bug larva, feeler (Pyrrhocoris apterus).
Section of left feeler missing.
Found in Polesskoje, Ukraine. Painted in Zürich.
1990. 42cm x 29.7cm.

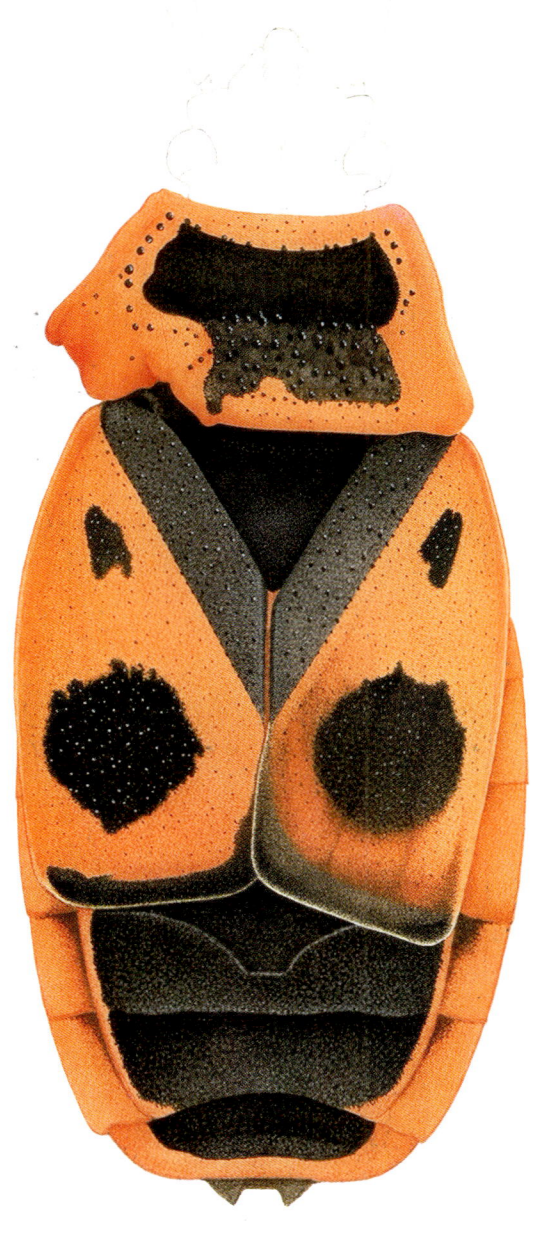

Fire bug (Pyrrhocoris apterus).
Left side of neckplate is deformed. The black spots are not symmetrical.
Found in Séljony Mys, near Checkpoint Charlie (within the 30km Chernobyl exclusion zone). Painted in Zürich.
1991. 42cm x 29.7cm.

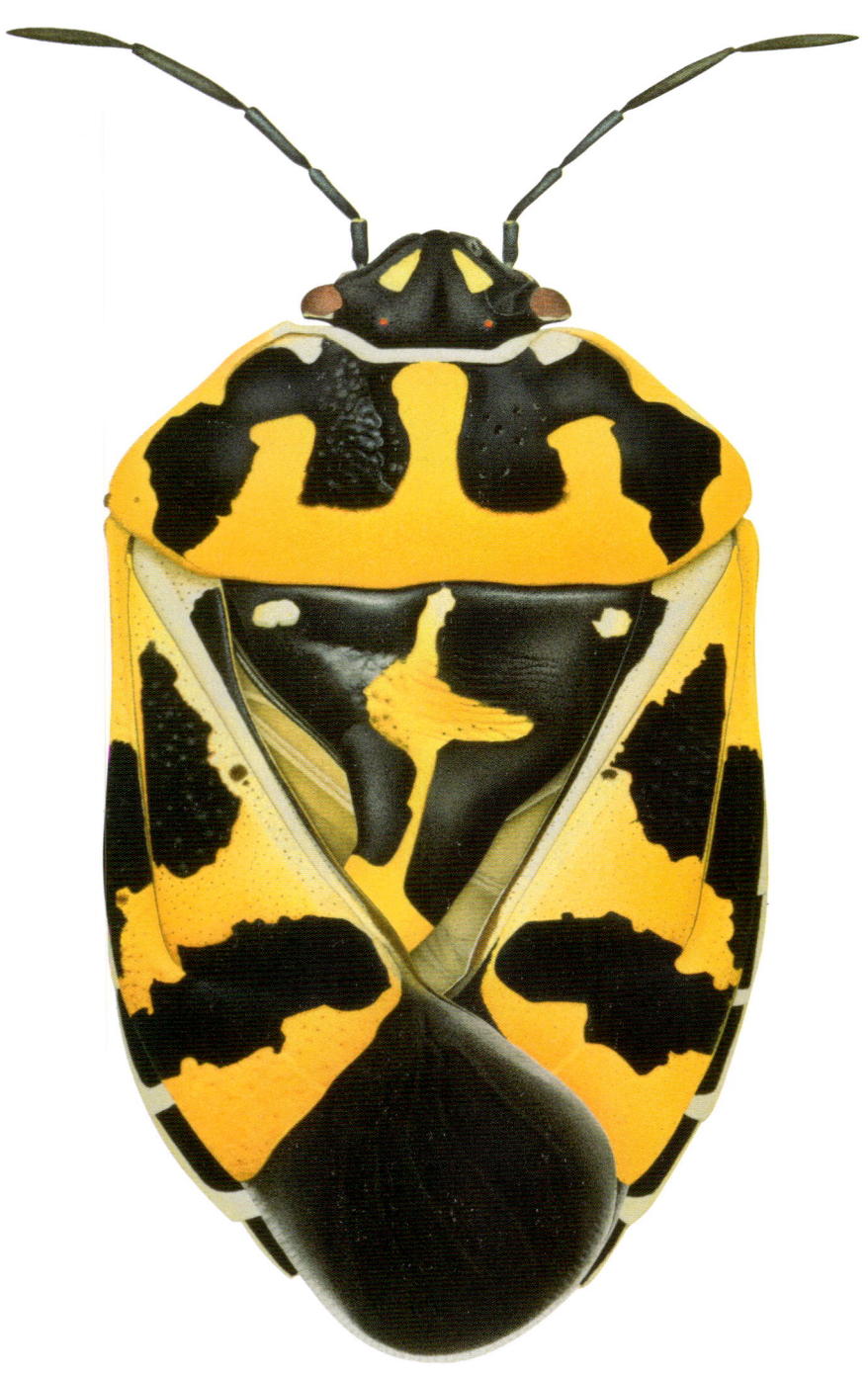

Harlequin bug (Pentatomidae).
Deformed scutellum, and patches not symmetrical.
Found near the Three Mile Island plant. Painted in Zürich.
1991. 42cm x 29.7cm.

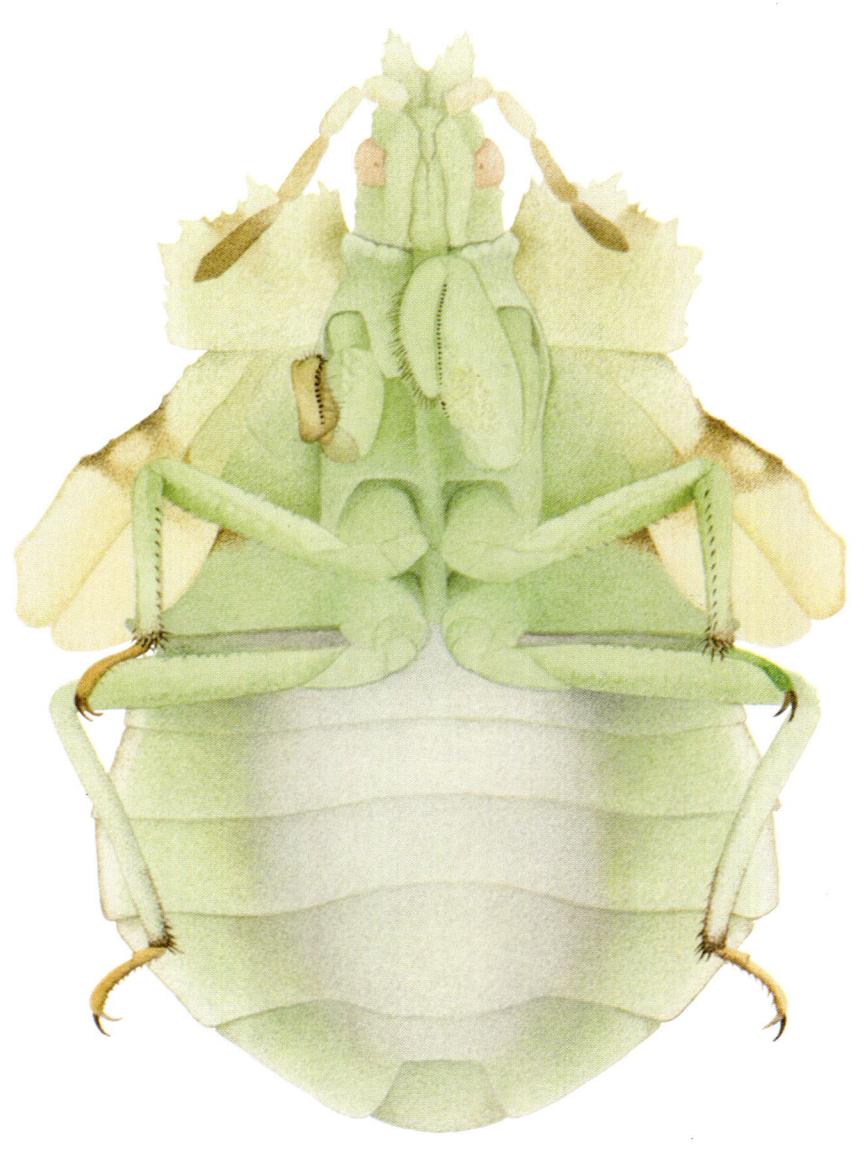

Ambush bug larva, top left leg (Phymatidae).
Short left front foot which is small with a brown dot.
Found near the Three Mile Island plant. Painted in New Cumberland.
1991. 42cm x 29.7cm.

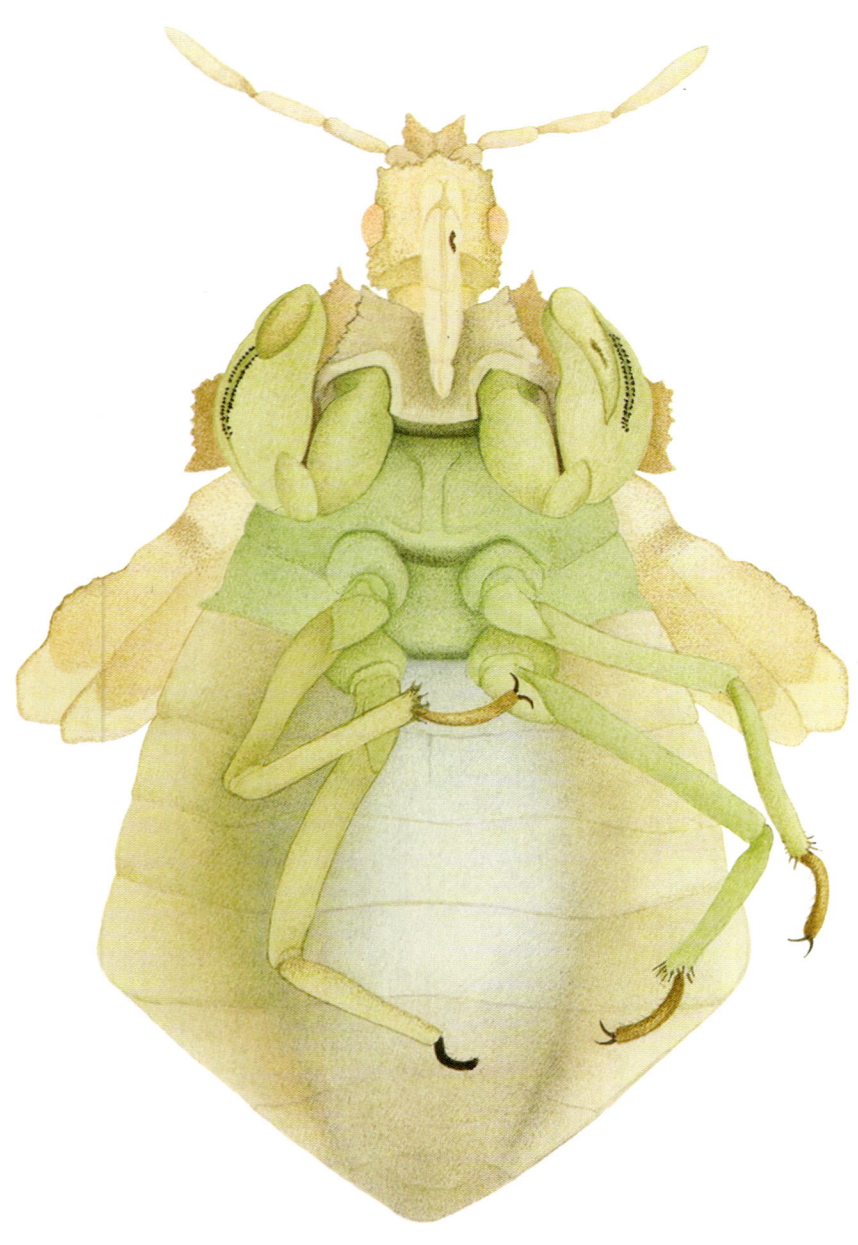

Ambush bug larva, bottom left leg (Phymatidae).
The legs go in every direction, the left hind leg is deformed and dark.
Found near the Three Mile Island power plant. Painted in New Cumberland.
1991. 42cm x 29.7cm.

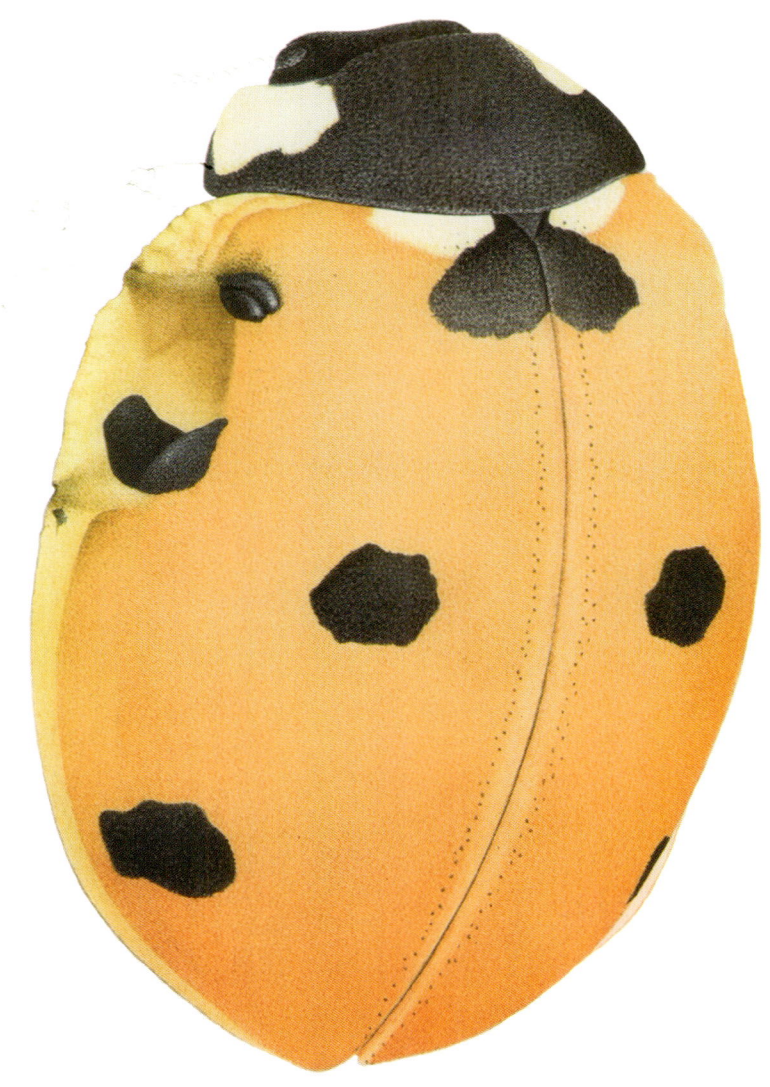

Ladybird (beetle family Coccinellidae).
A black growth rises from a depression, which reshapes the left wing.
Found near the Three Mile Island power plant. Painted in New Cumberland.
1991. 42cm x 29.7cm.

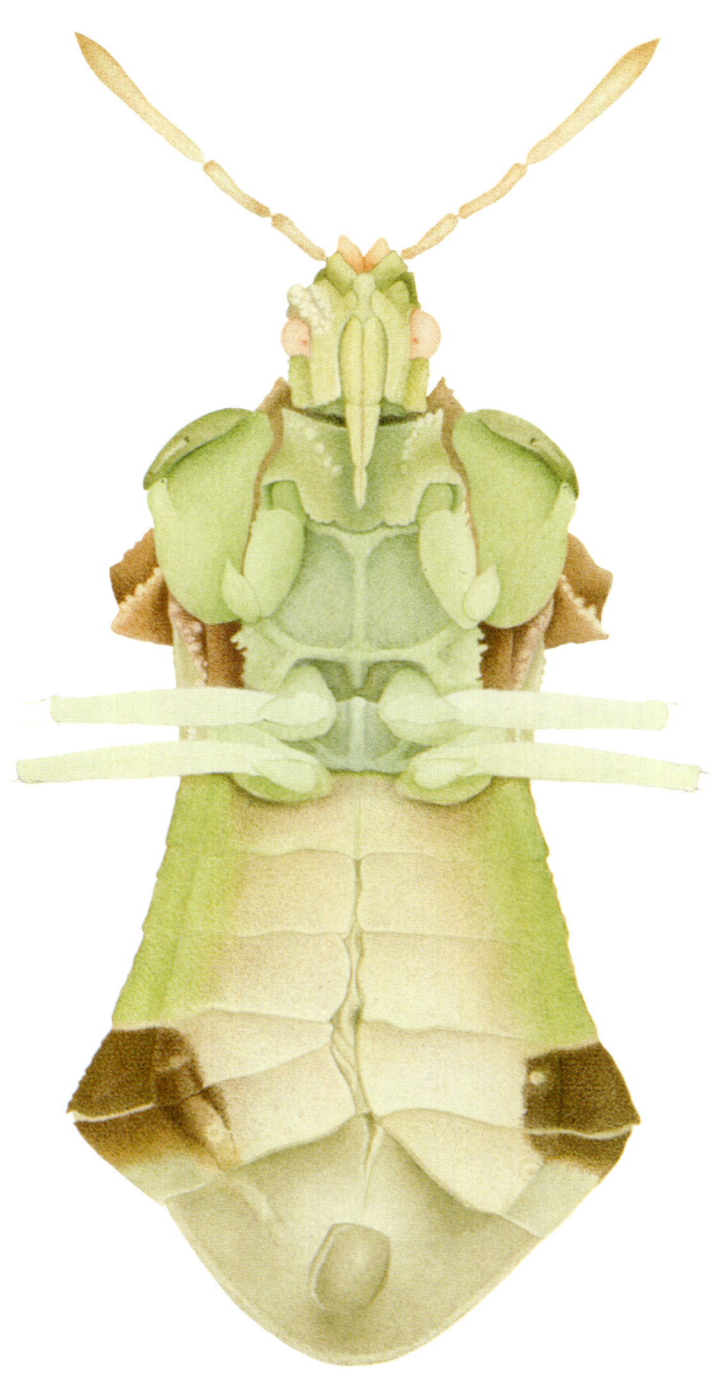

Ambush bug (Phymatidae).
The five segments on each side of the stomach are are unevenly formed and asymmetrically shifted.
Found near the Peach Bottom power plant. Painted in Zürich.
1991. 42cm x 29.7cm.

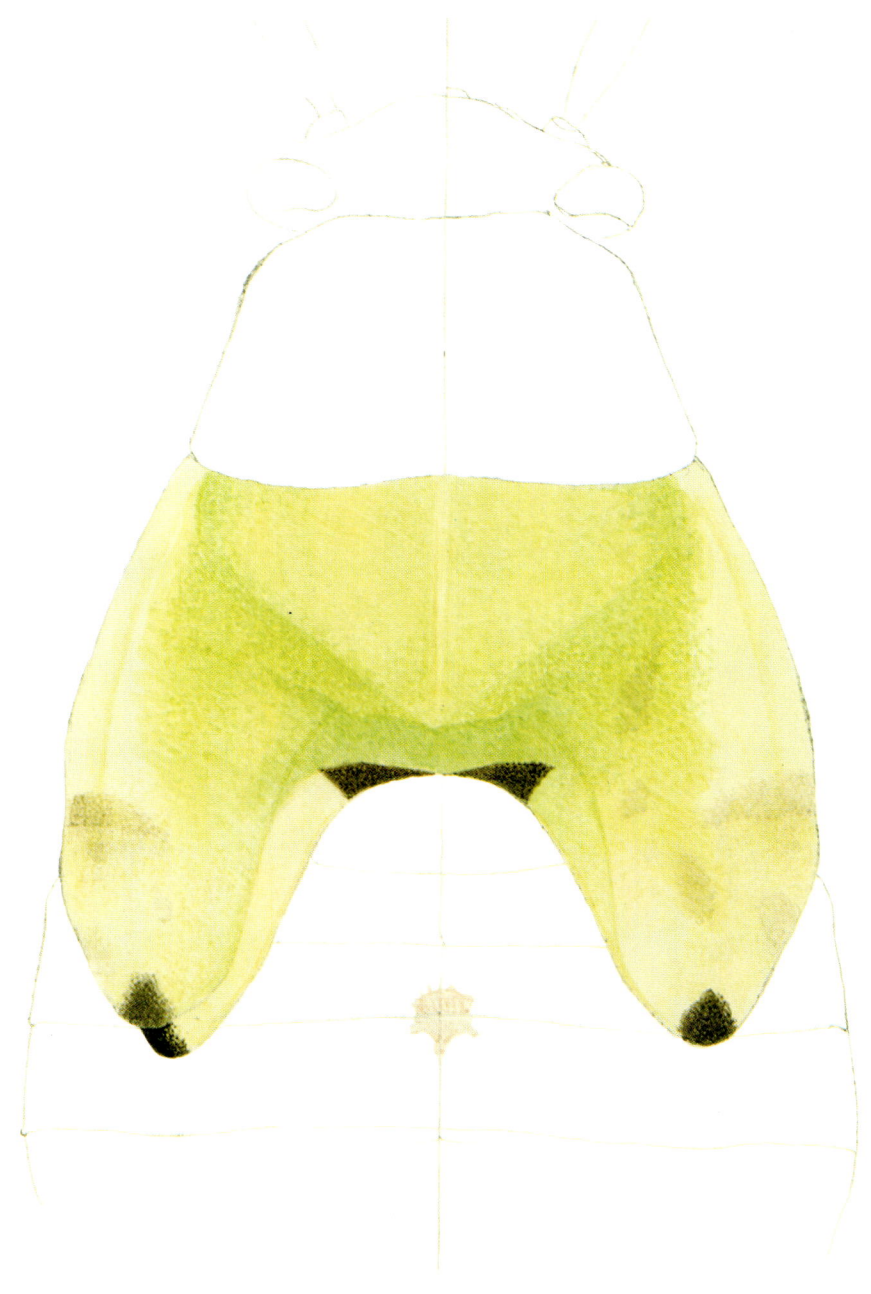

Soft bug larva (Miridae).
The left wings are divided, unlike the normal wings on right.
Found near Krümmel plant. Painted in Cuxhaven.
1995. 42cm x 29.7cm.

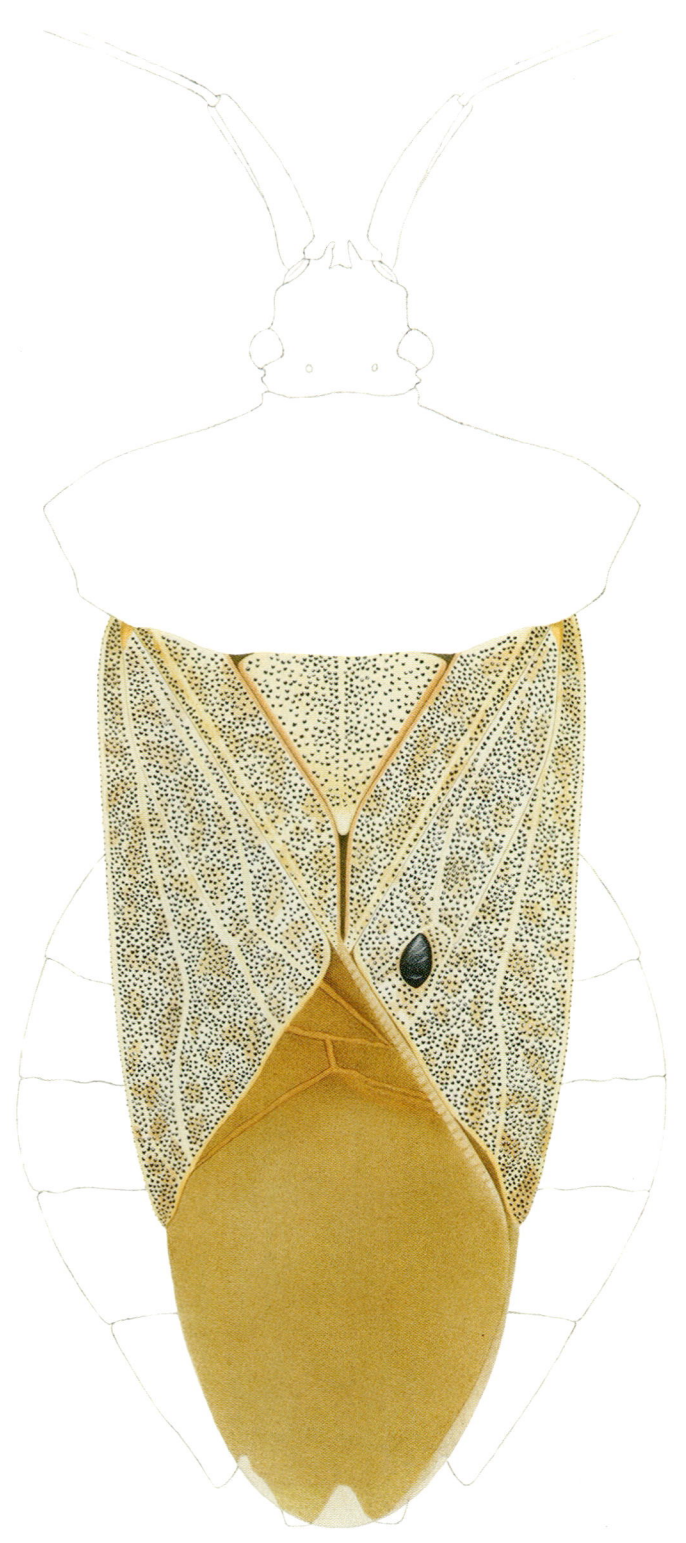

Squash bug (Coreus marginatus).
A black thick patch grows out of the wing
Found near Krümmel plant. Painted in Cuxhaven.
1995. 42cm x 29.7cm.

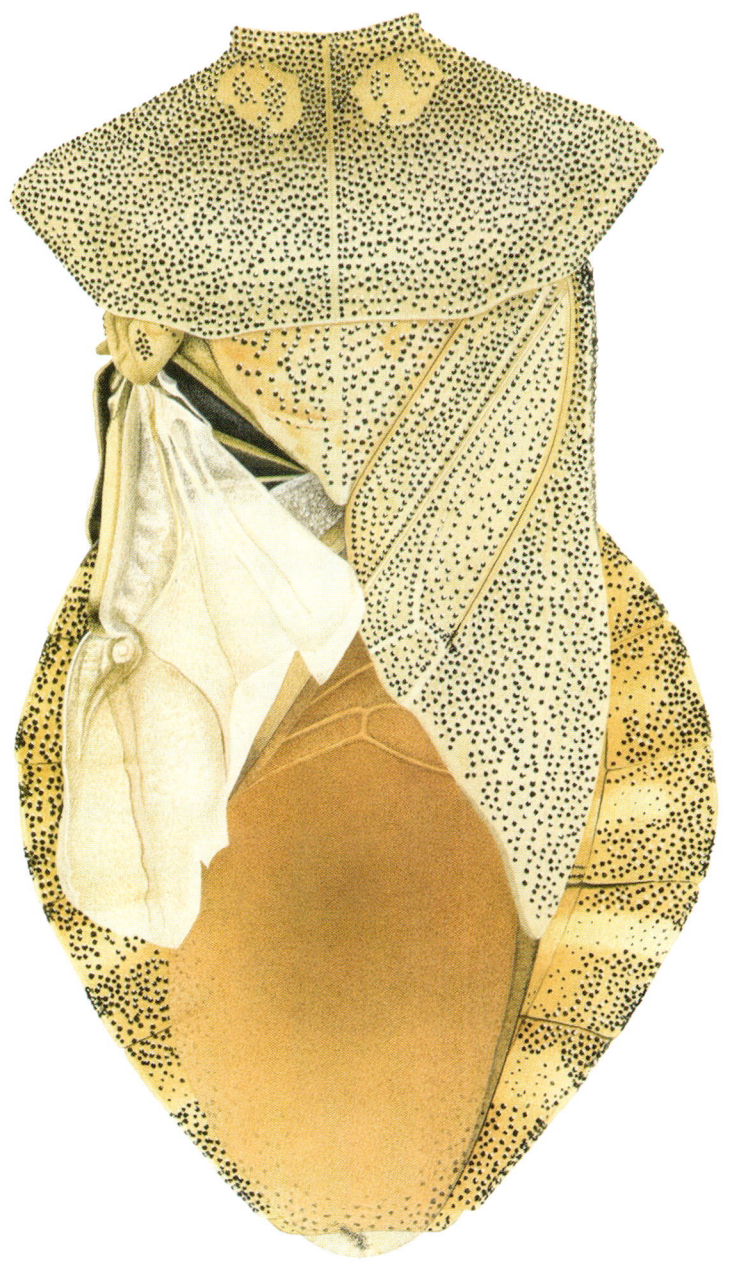

Squash bug (Coreus marginatus).
Left wing is tiny.
Found in Rohr. Painted in Zürich.
1995. 56cm x 76cm.

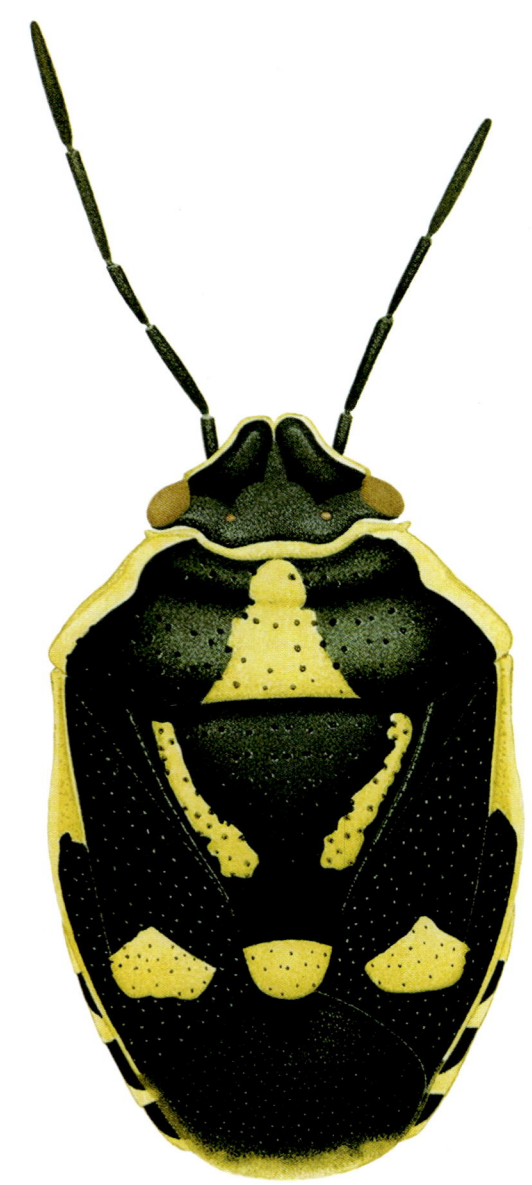

Vegetable bug (Eurydema oleraceum).
Section missing from right feeler.
Found in Rohr. Painted in Zürich
1995. 56cm x 76cm.

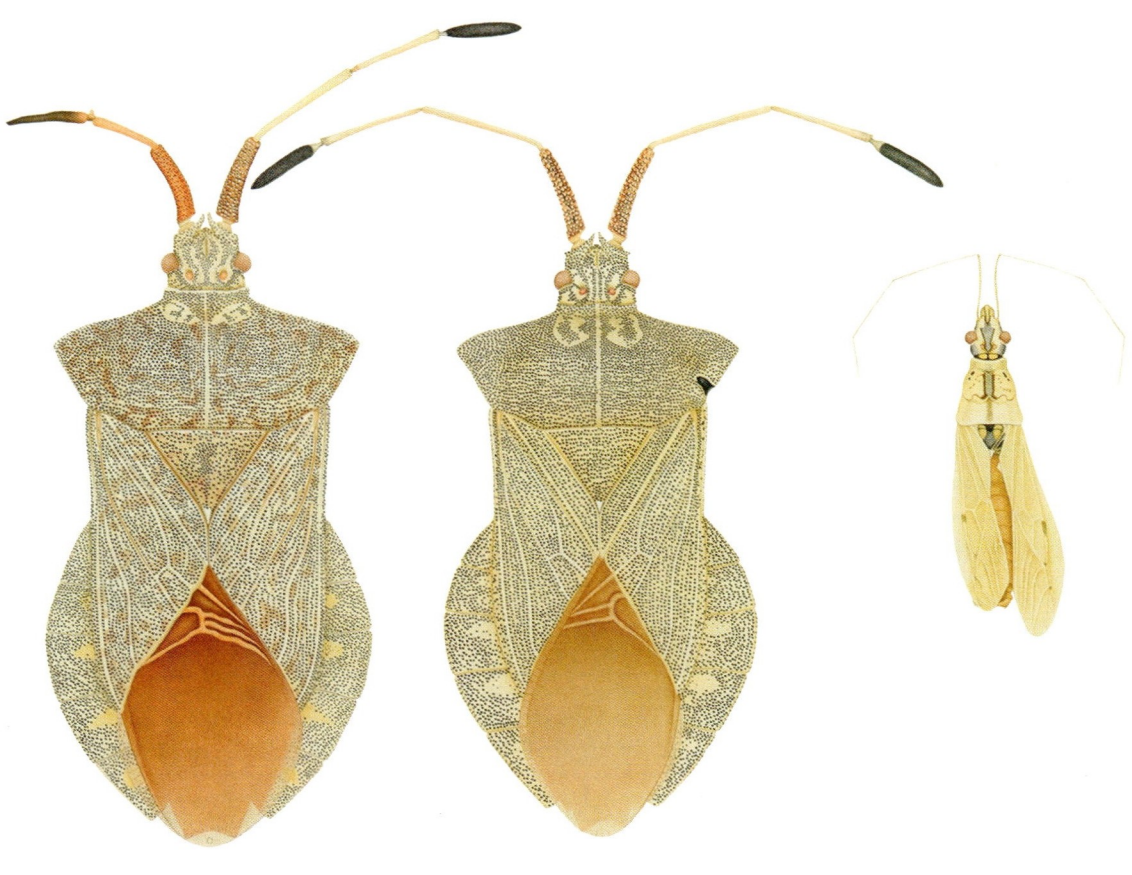

Three bugs (Coreus marginatus and Nabis rugosus).
The left squash bug has a section missing from the left feeler. The middle squash bug has a black
depression on the right side of the neckplate. The damsel bug on the right has wings of uneven length.
Found in Kleindöttingen. Painted in Zürich.
1996. 56cm x 76cm.